EVERYONE VERSUS RACISM

EVERYONE VERSUS RACISM

A LETTER TO MY CHILDREN

PATRICK HUTCHINSON

With Sophia Thakur

HarperCollins*Publishers*

HarperCollins*Publishers*
1 London Bridge Street
London SE1 9GF

www.harpercollins.co.uk

First published by HarperCollins*Publishers* 2020

3 5 7 9 10 8 6 4 2

A catalogue record of this book is
available from the British Library

ISBN 978-0-00-844399-3

Printed and bound in Great Britain by
CPI Group (UK) Ltd, Croydon

MIX
Paper from
responsible sources
FSC™ C007454

This book is produced from independently certified FSC™ paper
to ensure responsible forest management.

For more information visit: www.harpercollins.co.uk/green

To my children
Dominic, Tyler, Sidéna and Kendal.
To my grandchildren
Kyrie, Tiger-lily, Asia and Theo.
And one day to my great-grandchildren.
Everything I do is for you.

And to the greatest woman I've ever known
Maxine Adassa Prince ... my mum.

CONTENTS

INTRODUCTION

To my beloved children
and grandchildren,

After much thought, I have decided that a letter might best acquaint you with the times that I am living in. Textbooks have done enough damage to the truth, and a novel can often find itself mixing fact with fiction – much like the news channels of today. But a letter is the product of my heart being given a pen. Of course, my heart has become calloused – perhaps too much a product of what it has been subjected to. But its posture is an honest reaction to what life has apportioned to me. If I can promise anything, it is an honest reflection of what it has meant to exist in the twenty-first century – as a black person in a world that celebrates black suppression. As a black man in a world that seems to crave black men's blood. As a black person who is certain that compassion is the only solution to the deadly tale of racism. I am not saying that we should forgive and forget. But I believe that in our fight to move forward, we must arm ourselves with as much empathy as we do energy. I think that the only thing left that can save humanity is a touch more humanity from both sides. Many people will disagree with this position, and I do not blame them. After watching the video of George Floyd's murder, I, too, was filled with anger. In fact, sometimes the aching parts of me still are. Unfortunately, however, I've lived to see how consuming vengeance can become once empowered. I've worked in the martial arts my whole life and I know what can happen when rage justifies itself before searching for a peaceful solution. I've wished the revolutionary well on their way into a life of such activism. I know we need them. I know we cannot all be them. I desire to laugh truthfully, from the floor of my gut, with my radiant grandchildren, and fill their bodies with love and hope rather than anger and resentment.

Sometimes this means closing my heart when rage comes knocking. Shielding my young family from the structures that may one day work against them. Sometimes it means turning off the news, forcing my head deep into the waters of joy and trying to fish out a level of compassion and humanity that I wish was extended to me. Deep in the anatomy of the black being, there is a resource so rare in the fallen world. Something that has perhaps had to be conditioned into us so we can survive. Hope. A grieving, electric hope for a more balanced tomorrow.

I have decided to write a letter because, since the beginning of time, letters have preserved the truth of the moment, even if that truth has changed by the time the ink dries. If all this shard of my heart does is to project the current state of affairs beyond our WhatsApp group chats and kitchen tables, it has played its part in commemorating a season of life that I hope changes the world. Goethe, an eighteenth- and nineteenth-century writer, referred to a letter as an 'immediate breath of life'. Today, the streets scream 'I can't breathe' into a mourning sky, repeating the last words from several black men who have been brutally killed at the hands of the police. We hold signs, take to the streets and pull fire from our throats. We eternalise the last words of these men by forcing them into the everlasting journey of the wind, in the hope that we keep breathing long enough to see our grandchildren scream only in laughter, and not in protest.

Perhaps you will stumble across this manuscript years from today, during a time when letter writing no longer serves as a form of documentation. Maybe your fingertips will pause on the spine of this book and you will tug on its skin till it slips from its shelf into curious palms. You might push the dust away with your breath, rotate it between your fingers and begin to digest the blurb on the back cover. And as you get to the last line, you might wonder whether the year 2020 was fiction or non-fiction. As I piece together this letter, I wonder the same. Living, or at least surviving, has begun to feel like an existential satire. In an attempt to convince my body that it is not an actor in *The Truman Show*, I write obsessively about the times, hoping to make sense of the pandemic we have found ourselves in. No, not COVID-19. A much older disease. Racism.

I have worn black skin for centuries. And over these years my flesh has been weaponised, regulated, discriminated against, bleached, incinerated, sold and yet, somehow, I have survived. Somehow, I smile. But you won't remember me from my smile. You will remember me from a photograph that forced a large percentage of the watching world to pause. To stop thinking for long enough to question their thoughts. To question their bias and decide how they felt towards a six-foot-one black man lifting a barely breathing white man from beneath blood-stained shoes and carrying him to the feet of police officers who picked their other, arguably less essential job of documenting the violence for evidential purposes (as opposed to stopping the incident) on their selfie sticks and smartphones. Depending on which side of favour you fall, the thought of a police officer not doing their duty to defuse the violence and protect the violated may seem appalling, if not felonious, during a moment such as this. But by 2020, this hardly came as a surprise to me, a black man. A black man who believes that if life and death cannot discriminate, then nor can we begin to play master over who deserves to live or die. On that Saturday, near Waterloo Station, when I saw a man's breath being robbed from him by righteous rage, I saw only a man. One whose death would scatter a family, but also tarnish the Black Lives Matter movement in a way that I knew we could not afford. Not after such a global display of peaceful, progressive momentum.

The centuries have shown this compassionate position to be held time and time again, almost exclusively by the victims of those who kill to hone their omnipotence. Perhaps, as black people, we have no choice but to be graceful. To suppress our anger and pray that in our peace, we can remind the world of our shared humanity – even though, like animals, we are still hunted and killed for our skin, despite our imposed demureness.

Across my TV screen in the weeks leading up to this particular protest, I and the rest of the world watched graphic videos of the police killing innocent black people. We saw how our worth was valued. We waited for verdicts on indictments or arrests that never came. We watched children's innocence become a life of protest during the short time it took for a policeman to suffocate someone's daddy.

We watched the worry grow on our own mothers' faces as history continued to hurt. We wondered why, for centuries, white people felt entitled to our very breath. The wonder mobilised and we took to the streets to convince everything under the global sky that black lives mattered just as much as any other. But the unambiguous objectivity of a united quest towards equality sent a shiver down racist spines.

When you've held power for so long, equality will look like oppression.

An anti-Black Lives Matter protest was announced by the English Defence League co-founder Tommy Robinson (who we will talk about a bit later) in the middle of the biggest global movement towards equality. A spear was fired into the black body, in the hope that it would stop the world from running into a better tomorrow. To be anti-Black Lives Matter is not only to suggest that black people do not deserve equality. When the catalyst to this protest was a pandemic of black men being unfairly slaughtered, to contest the movement is to support the legalising of black murder. And in the hundreds of white people who came out that weekend to reveal the true tarnished nature of their racist hearts, we saw Britain. Together they chanted racist chants as they marched the streets of London, stomping on the tender hearts that had lined the roads and stripping England of its progressive facade. In doing so, the Western world was reminded that not only is there so much work to do, there is also an equal amount of discriminatory work to un-do.

That Saturday, fathers told their children to stay home. These dads, like myself, had lived through senseless white rage before and knew how aggressive it could be. Mums forbade their daughters from attending the original protest planned for that day because they, too, knew what angry, empowered racist men were capable of. But us? We knew we had to be there. If not to protect the momentum of these protests, then to protect our black boys who refused to be silenced by white men. I didn't expect to find a white man gasping for breath slung over my shoulders. I'm sure he didn't imagine surviving at the hands of the race he came out to fight against. I definitely didn't expect the footage of me potentially saving his life at the anti-black protest to go viral.

But what has shocked me the most is how one transformative image can have the power to break and recast a narrative.

CHAPTER 1

IN THE BEGINNING

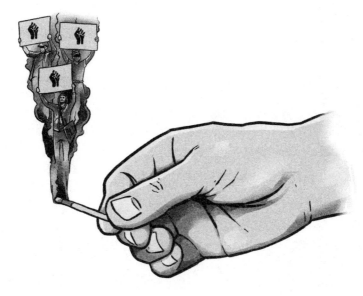

'We hold signs, take to the streets and pull fire from our throats … in the hope that we keep breathing long enough to see our grandchildren scream only in laughter, and not in protest.'

One day years from now, in a history lesson, a classroom of children will be asked to create a poster that they think accurately captures the events of 2020. If each student does not find their yellow, red and orange markers, and begin sketching a huge flame across a blank piece of paper … I will know that, once again, the textbooks have lied. A match was lit against the spine of 2020 and we watched our great plans for the new year flicker under a smoky sky. By March it seemed like the world had caught fire. We watched from our living rooms as the skies were emptied of planes, the earth had space to exhale, and colour and class raged against each other as if it were the sixties. Some of us thanked the higher powers that a global pandemic had chained us to our houses and made the decision for us to sit this race war out. Many people wanted to turn face masks into muzzles, mark their doors and keep their heads down, hoping that both the Black Lives Matter movement and COVID-19 would pass them by. But something was different this time. A mirror had been held up to the face of the earth and the open wounds that turned smiles into tears had never been more apparent. Especially when those tears became blood spilt from black eyes.

Extra melanin has meant extreme mistreatment for longer than I've been alive. We could be talking about the caste system in India that favours lighter skin while quite literally killing those with darker skin. We could be talking about the Arab media that only celebrates pale tones, or the film roles of the slave, prostitute, villain or thug, which are exclusive to darker brown skin. We could even be talking about the millions of children's doll collections that are created everyday, each with white skin, rosy lips, long straight hair and European facial features. The world is wrapped in favouritism towards whiter skin, whether we care to admit it or not.

And despite global efforts to address this post-colonial pandemic, we have all built our lives and minds around this reality. This is particularly true for the police departments that are paid to protect the land. Somewhere in the DNA of the police officer, it seems an active wire of racism snaps and goes wild within them when faced with the opportunity to either serve a harmless black person their rights or kill them. The statistics are not pretty. In fact, they are truly terrifying. According to Statista, as of August 2020, for every one million US citizens, thirty-one unarmed black citizens are shot and killed by the police – the highest rate for any ethnicity. To know that my last breath lies in the hands of a volatile and highly emotional human being who feels justified in both discriminating against me and murdering me … it's a very disheartening hand to have been dealt along with my mother's black skin.

Perhaps you come to find this letter at a time when race is only celebrated, and not used to determine whether a person lives or dies. Perhaps you struggle to believe that humans could ever kill other humans because they look different to them. Perhaps your heart has evolved to the point that my heart, and millions of other tired hearts, reached centuries ago. So maybe this seems far-fetched to you. If you're reading this even ten years from today, I really hope it does. I hope you're filled with disgust, doubt and curiosity. But in the likely event that the textbooks and the statistics change, and the essays are lost, and the artists get tired of the truth, and the news moves on and the silver lining becomes the entire picture of 2020, here's the truth of today …

Black people are still getting killed for being black. The killers sometimes become celebrities. In the case of George Zimmerman, who fatally shot unarmed, innocent seventeen-year-old Trayvon Martin in 2012, the killer becomes a hero, who has rid the street of another black future. Zimmerman went on to try to sue the family of Trayvon Martin, appear on news shows and begin a new career as a glorified killer. There was something about this particular killing, amid the many that took place that year, that split the ground beneath us. Before the blood had dried, the potency of witnessing the loss of a son and unarmed teenager, a grieving mother, a not-guilty verdict and an acquitted killer unearthed a twentieth-century rage that seemed to come from the belly of the civil rights movement. A video recording was released proving the innocence of Trayvon Martin and his cold-blooded killing by George Zimmerman. Yet somehow, a jury found him not guilty. Somehow, a video of the events was just not enough. Somehow, the law was put aside and Trayvon Martin's parents had to watch their son's killer become a celebrity. The right side of the world shook with rage. With helplessness. With confusion. Then we shook into formation. The Black Lives Matter movement was created by Alicia Garza, Patrisse Cullors and Opal Tometi as a response to the staggering number of innocent black deaths across the world. Unfortunately, all of the press, all of the support and all of the evidence since just hasn't been enough to stop the same thing from happening over and over and over again. It's tiring. And, if I'm completely honest with you, on the day of this protest that changed the world (hopefully for good), I was actually too tired of this vicious cycle to even leave my house. Had it not been for the mandem, perhaps you wouldn't be reading this letter. Here is what has led me, so led you, to this letter. An afternoon in London that completely transformed my life.

On the thirteenth day of the sixth month of an already very devastating year, we changed the world. Hopefully. Unintentionally. I didn't plan to. In fact, my own plan for that Saturday afternoon was to play with my two grandchildren, do some exercise and pray that the day's protest didn't go as horribly as many of us envisioned it would. We were at war again. They had killed another innocent black man. A video had gone viral of a police officer named Derek Chauvin pressing his knee onto the neck of George Floyd on the side of a road in Minneapolis, Minnesota, suffocating him without restraint, with his hands in his pockets, until George Floyd could no longer breathe and was killed. Passers-by screamed and watched. Other officers watched and filmed. Derek Chauvin looked into the lens of the camera and kept his knee on George Floyd's neck for over eight minutes. Even those who somehow found an excuse for every police killing could not excuse this graphic murder of George Floyd. A father, son and friend to many. Due to a medical pandemic that had everyone strapped to their sofas, working from home and being online more than ever before, the video went viral very quickly and demanded the attention of just about everyone with a heart. For some, this was their first sight of how blatant racism could be. For many of us, though, we were hurt but not shocked. As a black man who's grown up in a predominantly white London, I've known how vicious racism can be from a very young age. That's why my friend called me on that Saturday morning, begging me to attend what was meant to be a peaceful BLM protest, had it not been for the propaganda that Tommy Robinson had infected the air with.

The overtly racist and hugely problematic EDL party leader Tommy Robinson released a video encouraging football hooligans, thugs and anti-black people to disrupt the peaceful Black Lives Matter protest. The video made me sick to my stomach. Not because of the hate speech. Or the blatant and unsubtle agenda to silence a movement that finally seemed to be impacting on those who needed to bring about change. But because of what it exposed about how part of Britain's heart feels towards black people's survival. My gut twisted itself into a fist of rage. And while I'm a trained martial artist who knows how to channel that anger with wisdom without inviting arrest (not that you have to do much as a black man), this isn't the case for many of us. And I get it. How dare this white man unleash his dogs on our protest? How dare he trigger our people at a time such as this? The blood is still wet. For many people, deciding not to protest would be feeding their oppression. And so the hundreds that still came out that day and screamed louder and marched harder, they refused to let a white man win. My friend had watched the video of Tommy Robinson and knew this was bad news. He empathised with the black protesters who would still leave their houses that morning and face the racists head on. My friend was well aware of how dangerous rage could be once it is reciprocated. It wasn't a fate he wanted for anybody. Least of all vulnerable black people.

When he called me that morning, I asked why he felt we needed to do this. He's a spiritual man and he said he had felt nudged by his ancestors to put his career in security to good use in this way. To go out there and protect those who needed protecting, since we all knew the police had no intention of doing so. This completely resonated with me.

Between the six of us guys who ended up heading out to the protest that Saturday afternoon, two of us worked in security and all of us were trained in martial arts. Defence was what we were built for. Protection was more than a job. It was our duty as able-bodied, well-trained black men to step into ourselves on that day. Yes, however, was not my first response. In fact, it was quite the opposite. I'm sure I started by saying no. Not because I didn't think we needed to do this, but because I had my grand-children nestled in between my bicep and forearm, and anybody who has held a baby knows how impossible it is to leave them once those little angels have found comfort in your presence. Like my mother before me, I feel entirely obligated to my role as a protector of these cubs. I didn't grow up with a father present. In fact, thanks to him, I spent years assuming I had no older men in my life at all beyond my uncle and his friends – only to find that this wasn't the case. But that's a story for another letter. Maybe this was what would get me off the sofa and take me into my room to find a face mask and some gloves. Perhaps it was the desire that lives in any son who grew up without a dad that forced me to find my feet and be a better example of leadership. Or maybe it was seeing how safe and blissful my grandchildren were when they were around me. Perhaps something of that security reminded me of how safe I felt as a twelve-year-old when I spent time with my uncle Charles and his friends. I felt brave when I was with them. Like nobody could disrespect us. I was proud of my blackness and loved being one of many. It's a real shame to then learn when you grow up that even though I felt so warm in the centre of blackness, to onlookers we were an immediate threat. I became sure that those who did feel threatened by collective blackness were probably the same people who would turn up to antagonise the protesters. Why did they hate us this much? We weren't even protesting for equality. Simply just to matter, and not be killed.

My friend and I exchanged a heavy silence on the phone. I could feel how sure he was that we needed to be there. His spirit man had already seen the number of lives we would save that day, and who am I to argue with his God? I looked down at my grandchildren and my heart tightened. Perhaps if I went out to protect the Black Lives Matter image today, they wouldn't have to march tomorrow for the exact same, tired reasons. Maybe in protecting the mothers and children in the streets today, I was protecting these adorable black seeds of mine. Maybe by putting them down today, I was actually lifting them up for tomorrow. Quite quickly, my maybes became definitelys and I kissed the little angels on their precious foreheads and stretched my fatherly heart around London. After all, everyone deserves someone who's dedicated to protecting them. And if the police won't, the people should. Well … at least the trained, strong, present-minded people should. That's what my friend thought, anyway. I wasn't the first person he called who said no. Some of the guys he tried refused to play the role of policemen after all that the force had put our people through. Some were tired of having to be the good guys all the time and others genuinely feared that this was a deadly set-up. But the six of us who went to the protest that day weren't thinking about our own lives. At least, not in a fearful sense.

As we made our way towards the protest, we were confident in our skills and our ability to defuse situations and protect the vulnerable. My friend, Jamaine, Sean and I drove past Parkway and parked in Vauxhall. My friend and I in one car, Jamaine and Sean in the other. We met Lee and Chris at Vauxhall Station. I'm familiar with the area, so I knew where we could park without getting a fine or our wing mirrors knocked off. Walking across the bridge from Vauxhall, we saw the first signs of what we were heading into. There were smaller groups of EDL men standing around. They were looking at us and we were looking at them. We all knew exactly what it was between us. We knew why they had come out to disrupt a Black Lives Matter protest, and I guess they assumed we'd come to stop them. The air thickened, our throats tightened and we shared a long, deep exhale as we headed towards Parliament Square. The day resembled a carnival in some ways. It felt like we were walking for ages and some of the boys went off on their own to see what was happening, and where it was happening. Once we had all come back together, we ended up back at Vauxhall and thought it best to get on a train towards Piccadilly. As four or five of us climbed into the carriage, it was as if the world paused for a moment. There were EDL anti-black protesters and football hooligans already taking up space on the train. They looked at us in a funny way. My friend Jamaine described it as how an animal looks at its prey while it's waiting for the perfect time to attack. There was a strong sense of 'not here, but later' oozing from the stares and whispers of the white men.

After all the convincing that my friend had had to do, we were actually a bit late to the protest, ironically feeding the stereotype of black men's poor timing. But in our defence, in that short window of time we'd had to find sitters for our children and protective outfits to change into. We got to the square at around 2.30 p.m., and by this point there were roadblocks and redirections everywhere. Police officers kept telling us to go this way or that way, or that the path ahead was blocked. We made a point of remaining polite when talking to the police, aware of our huge physiques and dark skin. Thankfully the police made a point of doing the same. If only this were the norm. Better yet, if only we didn't have to consider how to act innocent, without ever having committed a crime. As we walked towards Trafalgar Square, we passed smaller groups of anti-black protesters who always made a point of nodding their heads at us or breaking the tension with a 'You good, bruv?' The greeting became an attempt at a white flag. Perhaps to say that they weren't trying to antagonise us. On a normal day I'd enjoy

nodding back and returning it. But today, despite how desperate a white man might be to break the tension, I couldn't shake the fact that he'd come here on Saturday on the thirteenth day of the sixth month, for a reason that I really struggle to digest.

By the time we got to Trafalgar Square, our six had become five. One of our boys was tired of walking, and I didn't blame him. I had to keep reminding myself why we had come, and why it was worth leaving my grandchildren. Although London that Saturday did not let us forget why we came. As we got closer and closer to the body of the march, on every corner we turned there was a new group of football hooligans or white thugs throwing bottles at the police or chanting racist slurs into a wind that was meant to carry the voice of peaceful black protest. With each step into this dark, twisted moment, it became terrifyingly clear that the anti-Black Lives Matter protesters wanted violence. They were itching for the opportunity to crack open their bodies and launch their prejudices into the spirit of London. They wanted to see the black man snap and they wanted the media to see it, too.

From behind a wall of police, a mob of white men screamed non-rhythmic chants and slurs towards a sea of black people who were waiting patiently for them to finish so that they could continue to fight for their right to survive. This really wasn't what the Black Lives Matter protesters needed that day, while innocent people were being killed on camera at the hands of police across the world. The mob screamed everything from 'We are racist, yes we are' to 'Black lives don't matter'. They stretched their hateful necks above the police, who protected them from the consequences that were naturally brewing in the bellies of the BLM protesters. And they screamed. They broke the wall of silence that tends to protect the ignorant opinions of those who are adamant that racism doesn't exist. They screamed louder than that denial. They screamed and woke Britain up to its racist side. They screamed in the hope that if one of those screams could pierce through enough black ears, a riot would occur.

And if they could get the black people to the point of fighting, the media would quickly remember only the violence that came from the protests. Oh, the luxury of knowing one's privilege.

At the square we bumped into quite a few people we knew. Stories from the day poured from their lips, and we pieced together a picture of the protest so far. As they told us of the smaller fights that kept breaking out like little fires across London, the square began to de-mist and became a showreel of the things they were saying. They became narrators of a scene in which we had all become actors. That's what it felt like. A movie. Usually, when racism is this destructive, it is subtle. It's in the micro-aggressions in the workplace or the inaccurate school curriculum. Today it shone with the sun and burnt any doubt I may have had off of my back. The racism was raw. Loud. Undeniable. From any angle, you could see smaller squabbles breaking out between drunk white football hooligans and the Black Lives Matter protesters. It was beginning to look like a ticking time bomb, and the police knew this, too. We all knew that at any given moment, a full-blown brawl could commence. Most of the Black Lives Matter protesters had never been in a brawl before, nor had they left the house that morning with any intention of fighting. The same could not be said for everyone. The jaws of the anti-black thugs gnashed like fighter dogs waiting to be unleashed. The police knew that if they did not bring this protest to a close, and quickly, anarchy would break out.

Around 5 p.m. they began to usher us all towards Waterloo Bridge. As everyone walked over the river, I'm sure some very dark thoughts crossed the minds of some of the anti-Black Lives Matter protesters as they funnelled down towards the station and the Southbank Centre. Between us guys, we had said that as long as we stayed vigilant and remained together, we would be okay. Although our initial aim was to protect the vulnerable Black Lives Matter protesters, we quickly realised that the right thing to do was protect anyone who was in harm's way. This included several anti-black disrupters. The point of all these protests was to make it clear that somebody's skin colour should not be the defining factor in whether they live or die. How, then, could we ignore it when a white man was left on his own to finish a fight that he might have started but would certainly lose, and possibly die from, if the situation was not defused? My natural instinct is to protect the vulnerable. When we saw a car carrying EDL thugs get stopped and sat on, we knew that if we didn't help them go home (and hopefully rethink their prejudice), they could become victims of the very abuse they had come out to serve. So we pulled people of all colours from the sides of the car and created a kind of open path for them to leave and never return. Although we didn't do this to make any kind of political point, I do secretly hope that they saw our faces. But even if they didn't, the next guy definitely did.

We followed the crowd towards Waterloo Station. I don't know who trains riot police, but ushering big, contending groups into one small, enclosed public area is definitely not something I would have done. From the bottom of the steps that separate the Southbank Centre and the Waterloo Station underpass, we noticed there was a conflict unfolding at the top of the stairs. From a martial arts perspective, this was hardly a place to stage any kind of fight, but drunk people do as drunk people please. And unfortunately for this drunk white man, his friends had left him to suffer the consequences of their racist monkey and slavery chants. He had it rough at the top of the stairs and we weren't the only black people to see what was happening through the lens of compassion. A black Rastafarian-looking man had intervened and was trying hard to protect the white thug's head. Between fights to the left and fights to the right, it all became too much too quickly for the black man in the middle and we knew we had to break this up before it worsened for both of the men.

I'm often asked why we felt the need to go and save this white man after all that he stood for in coming to disrupt a peaceful protest. The truth is, living with the image of a man being beaten to death is not something I could ever stomach. I don't know how the police do it so often. Perhaps it's the martial artist in me, or the father, or the security experts in my boys, but watching someone being beaten up till defeat isn't something we ever want to normalise. Regardless of colour. This isn't something we had to think twice about in that moment. Plus, if we had decided that it was okay for this man to potentially die, just because of his colour, how different would we have been from the very thing that the Black Lives Matter protests are about? Killing black people just because they are black. We also knew that all it would take was one major white casualty for the entire narrative to be changed and for Black Lives Matter to be demonised.

To protect the most vulnerable was our mission that day, and in that moment, this white man was outnumbered and noticeably drunk. He seemed to be slightly injured and completely non-reactive to what was happening around him.

The boys cleared a path towards the white man. For what felt like just a second, we had our arms around him protecting him from both black and white people who must have been angered by what he was saying before we arrived. The stairway was small. More and more people were coming into the station. Policemen, news reporters and people just trying to use the underground. Within seconds, we became crabs in a bucket. Skin to skin, shoulder to shoulder. It was getting harder to protect both him and ourselves as the crowd grew in both size and enthusiasm. In a moment of clarity I knew that if we all stayed there with him, we would all meet the same, sorry fate. The only wise option was to remove him and ourselves from the bustling crowd and put him behind the line of police officers who were just standing, watching. Almost as if they were waiting for a tragedy to occur. With little to no communication, the boys created a shield of arms over our heads, and in one giant swoop I picked him up and laid him across my shoulders. I couldn't tell you whether he was heavy or not, but he did give me all of his weight with a drunk, helpless willingness. I wonder if he knew I was black at this point. I wonder if I mattered to him at this point.

Taking small steps at a time, in an effort to shield me, the boys had to stomach some blows from protesters who weren't finished dishing it out, but this was minor in the grand scheme of things. I walked a few metres, laden with the man over my shoulders. Once the crowd eventually realised that my boys and I were there to defuse the fights, they chipped away. I bowed in front of the police to let the white man's body slide from my black shoulders, delivering him at the feet of the protectors of the land. As

I came up to eye level with the man whose job I had just done while he and his colleagues recorded the event with their police selfie sticks, he said, 'Well done.' I do not remember saying thank you. The boys and I moved on to the next squabble. Saving that man's life took precedence over how unimpressive the police were that afternoon, but it is still shocking to see the videos of police officers filming instead of saving lives. Even the white lives. Even in 2020, when I assumed nothing new could surprise me. Our response has made people wonder what kind of candidates the police force hires. If a policeman can strangle an innocent man to death in front of his team, or shoot a sleeping woman in her bed multiple times in front of colleagues and get away with it … we have to question what kind of character they are looking for when they hire. The job is to protect the people, but it seems as though that is merely an afterthought extended only to a select few.

Later, the five of us went to Chris's friend's restaurant, Eat of Eden on Coldharbour Lane, on the edge of Clapham. Over a vegan mix-up of plantain, chickpeas and quinoa, eaten outside, we finally found words for a day that had been more action than talking – which is ironic, really, because the nature of a protest is to talk until there is action. I had assumed. There was a quiet joy between us that didn't quite know how to reach our lips. We were pleased to have done some good. To have saved a few lives and hopefully changed some perspectives in the process. But heavy under our tongues, there were some truths that had been unearthed that day that aren't the kind you wish to swallow down with vegan goodness. Britain had shown its hidden face. Or perhaps a better way of putting it is that Britain had finally put a face to its embedded racism. To be so bold as to take to the streets with the sole purpose of disrupting a march that was created to save black lives is quite a chilling thing to do. Although this wasn't a point of conversation over dinner, we all felt the hatred at the protest and it's a very unsettling feeling to live with. Nevertheless, if there is one thing that black people can do well, it is finding pockets of joy in the garment of resistance. My sister Pauline helped with that when she called me, her voice sending fireworks of excitement rocketing through the phone.

'Check your phone, Pat, check WhatsApp.' Before I knew what Pauline was talking about, I assumed it must be a response to the WhatsApp message that I had posted to our siblings' group chat. 'Saved a white man's life today,' it read, and not much else. My children say I need to learn to message with more enthusiasm, but I'm more of a phone-call person. This wasn't what Pauline was talking about. This was way bigger than the siblings' chat. This was bigger than every single one of my group chats, in fact. Probably yours, too. Somehow, the press that had made their way down to the protest had got extraordinarily clear footage of me lifting this white guy to safety, and the images had begun to go viral.

Now, one thing to remember is that I'm forty-nine years old. Going viral wasn't a career option when I was growing up, so it has never been a huge desire of mine. I used Instagram for fitness videos and martial arts, and had around 1.9k followers, but that was all I used it for. Suddenly we were all sat around the table with our phones out like millennials, clicking the articles that people had been sending to us, and watching my number of Instagram followers grow at an exponential rate. The picture was causing a divide between protesters, but also replacing the images of any violence at the protest. I thought this was a good thing, ultimately. As a black man who has lived through women crossing the road when they see me, to unfair treatment by the police, to racist jokes everywhere from the playground all the way up to the workplace, I thought this was probably pretty good press for a black man. The vast majority of the people who sent me messages or shared the footage agreed. Sat at the table over dinner, we were a mix of excitement, because our local boy had gone viral, and relief that black people had been shown to do something positive, despite the outright racism we faced that day and every day. We finished our meals and prepared ourselves for the coming days, when the news channels would decide how they wanted to approach the thirteenth day of the sixth month of the year.

If I had a penny for every time I was asked if the white man got in touch to say thank you, I'd be a rich man. If I had a penny for every shocked expression that followed from me telling them I haven't heard a word back, I'd be even richer. What's funny is people's reactions to my reaction. I think people expect me to be angry or disappointed that he hasn't found a way to thank us for protecting his life. Even when I try to be, I just can't. The reason his life was saved wasn't for a photo opportunity or for white people to change their tone with us black men. It would be nice if they did, but in the heat of such a wild moment, the only thing I wanted to achieve was his survival. Once we did that, we moved on to the next person. Like most parents would admit, doing the right thing is often a thankless task, and I'm perfectly fine with that. Among my friends, we do joke about why we think he hasn't got in touch. I don't care to speculate, but the whole ordeal does remind me of my white childhood friends. The only time they seemed to have nothing to say was when it concerned racism towards black people. I'm not saying that this is the case here, but it does take me back to the deafening silence I lived through growing up on an estate.

CHAPTER 2
(MIS-)EDUCATION

'… if from a young age, before the seeds of division have had time to be watered, children could come to understand racism as something that should never be a natural response to difference …'

$\int$ ome say plan-tain, some say plan-tin. Some say Battersea, some say Clapham. What I can be sure of is that I grew up as a Caribbean boy on a council estate between Battersea and Clapham. Between racists and people who were as close as family ... literally. It's impossible to grow up on a council estate in seventies and eighties Britain and not have a million stories to tell – many of which would be hard to believe today. That being said, history is often hard to believe once the times have moved on. We look at our grandparents in disbelief that they could have ever lived through some of the things we learn about in school, and that they survived and somehow got on with life.

Sometimes the truth of the past only becomes real once we are able to trace its impact on today's world. Immigrant parents in the UK hoard plastic takeaway containers like gold because when they first came into

Mum and me.

this country they were unfamiliar with ready meals and microwave dinners, and the plastic Tupperware containers needed to store curry, oxtail and jollof rice were expensive. To this day, my mum saves her takeaway plastics like it's the sixties.

She would discipline us with more enthusiasm than was probably necessary, because she came to London at a time when, if you were a black man who misbehaved in public, you could die for it. 'If you don't hear, you will feel' is one of the many Caribbean proverbs that would spring to mind just before I would do something quite naughty – only to then feel the consequences afterwards, despite knowing better. What can I say? I was a curious lad. So were my friends on the estate. Just not curious enough to unpick why they behaved and believed as they did. I suppose that is a luxury afforded to those who have never had to look upon themselves through the lens of being 'different' or a 'minority'. My experience is loaded with the history of minority groups. For some, their history begins the day they are born into a privileged group. The world is their oyster.

As a child I had a white friend and I was his black friend – the black friend in whom his prejudice found an excuse to exist. If ever questioned about whether his belief system or language was racist, I would spring to mind and in this brief moment of introspection he would be comforted by our companionship. How could he be racist, when he loved to hang out with Patrick Hutchinson? The phrase 'I'm not [insert form of discrimination], I have a [insert victim of this discrimination] neighbour' is more than just a desperate defensive plea. It's actually a shared mindset that extends to almost every industry in the twenty-first century. Today, we see 100 per cent white boardrooms for sports where the majority of players are non-white, and the excuse for that disparity is often,

'Well, we've given *them* a window of opportunity, what more do they want?' Or, 'We aren't racist, we employ black cleaners.' There's still a strong sense of possession and supremacy present in these kinds of responses, as if black people aren't deserving of a level playing field, even though they exist as an equal member of the human race, not a lesser one. There's a lot to say on why black people are still perceived as the lesser race, and I blame a large part of this ignorance on education. Or rather the lack of it. My white friend would say some wild things because his parents would say racist things. I remember once standing by my white friend as his mum was in a full-blown, heated argument with a black lady on the estate. His mum was calling her every racial slur under the sun. Despite me standing right beside him, my friend did not flinch or excuse her, as I did when my mum would bring in Caribbean behaviour unprovoked. No, he stood and watched and listened and learnt that this was an appropriate way to treat black people. After the situation defused, his mum took us both by the wrist and marched us home. I wonder if she recognised that one of the hands she was holding was the same colour as the woman's she had just abused. Or whether she wondered for a second what that must have been like to hear as a black child. I know that she wasn't, but she could have been talking about my mother. The owner of my heart. Reducing my melanin-rich queen with a level of ridicule that I would never use to degrade another human being. As I walked into their house, I understood for the first time why my mother wouldn't let us stay at or even visit just anybody's house. They couldn't ever be home to us. The walls had probably heard so many hateful words towards my skin colour that they would make the ceiling collapse on my little black body should I ever put a foot out of line. It wasn't safe for Pauline or me.

My mum knew this before I did. I can only imagine how many times she had to internally work out whether

Me, Mum and Pauline.

a friend of my friend's family was racist before deciding whether I could play with them. I wonder how she came to trust our elderly white neighbours Nil and Don. I wonder whether it was simply borne of necessity. My mum had to work around the clock, meaning somebody had to be there to look after us when she wasn't there. Nil and Don became Mum's guardian angels, taking us in and keeping us safe while she went out to earn the money to keep the lights on. Pauline and I didn't always like going to stay with them. We thought they carried the musty scent of old people.

I wish that was the reason I didn't like going to other white people's houses. I wish it was always something as trivial as smell, and not something as serious as racism. I'm not sure I even realised how bad racism was as a young boy. I knew I didn't like the feeling, but I'm not sure if I knew how wrong it was. As a boy, I cared to the degree that a child could care, while maintaining some level of innocence about the world's pitfalls. However, as an adult, I can't begin to tell you how frequently I've had to ask myself the exact same questions my mother had to ask. Before travelling, I have to consider whether the country is safe for a black man and his family. Before letting myself enjoy any job, I've had to put the office through my own probation stage to determine how much of my blackness would be accepted there. It's a reduced

way to live, having to work out the depth of the stereo-
typed view somebody may have of you. Is it
they-only-see-black-people-when-reported-on-the-news
bad, or they-come-from-a-racist-family bad? When it's
the latter, perhaps because of what I lived through as a
boy, I'm often aware that transforming their mindset will
be an uphill struggle. Because it's not enough to tell them
that a statement they've made is offensive. What's worse
about racism that is passed down the bloodline is that
each generation believes that the crazy stereotypes they
apply to black people in their own communities and
abroad are absolutely, undeniably factual and without
exception. They feel confident believing in these regres-
sive and aggressive stereotypes because every structure
around them suggests that they are, in fact, true.

If all that was taught in school was that Africa needed
European intervention because the place was full of
uneducated savages, and then as the school children
grew up they never saw a black teacher or banker or
politician, they would live believing that the reason for
this was because black people just weren't as smart as
other races. Christopher Columbus, the pirate, wrote a
letter to Spanish monarchs Ferdinand and Isabella in
1493, having returned from several islands in the
Caribbean. In this letter, he wrote candidly and with
disturbing pride about the possessions he had stolen

from the unsuspecting islanders. He wrote of how hospitable the inhabitants were once their fear had been tricked away. 'They are by nature fearful and timid. But when they see that they are safe, and all fear is banished, they are very guileless and honest, and very liberal of all they have. No one refuses the asker anything that he possesses.' Further down the letter, as he continues to describe the people as a man might describe an animal, he writes, 'As soon as I had [come] into this sea, I took by force some Indians from the first Island, in order that they might learn from us.' This is why I refer to him as a pirate. Piracy is defined as the act of 'robbery or criminal violence by ship or boat', and there's little doubt that this is what Columbus did.

For as long as the relationship between Europeans and 'others' has existed, the notion of superiority has been preserved in tandem, through the language used in text-books, the perverting of affirmative action and the media. If, on television, the portrayal of black people is restricted to the role of thugs, prostitutes or poor single mothers, and then the only time a black face is broadcast on the news is in a report on black-on-black crime or abuse of some sort (be that domestic or drug-related), the watcher – who may never have sat down and had a conversation with a black person – could very well go on living their life in fear of black people.

42

There was a very popular British sitcom that we would watch as a family growing up in the seventies. My mother, Pauline and I would throw our heads back and laugh at some of the jokes that were made. Today, when we watch back some clips from the show, our heads fall into our worn-out palms. Not because we've only just realised how racist the jokes actually were, but because these portrayals of black people have tattooed themselves across the minds of many older white people who haven't since opened them to a more accurate portrayal of blackness. The show was called *Till Death Us Do Part*, and the main character, Alf Garnett, was not a huge fan of black or gay people. One day his wife hired somebody to help around the house. He was black and he was gay. And both of these attributes quickly became the butt of every joke for that season. Recently I stumbled across a clip from the show and could not believe how normal it was to exude racism and homophobia in such a blatant way. As my blood began to bubble watching it, I had to tell myself that nobody knew any better at the time. That things were different then. I can only find so much comfort in that thought, because then I remember that these same attitudes towards black people (and gay people) continue to exist in the twenty-first century.

One day, ask your black male friends how often they hear car doors lock as they walk past a car. Ask them how many times people have crossed the road to avoid passing them. Ask them how many chins have lowered or fake phone calls have been made to avoid eye contact. Ask your black female friends how many times they've been asked if their father is in their life. Ask the black female boss how often she's been asked whether the business that she has created is actually her own. And then ask them both how many times they've overcompensated on their British accent to avoid judgement on their culturally charged tongue. Ask the black man how many times he's had to crack a black race joke or laugh at one to break a layer of white ice. Ask the young black accountant how many times he's had to show his ID to get into his own building in comparison to his white colleagues. Ask him how often he's been pulled over for no other reason than being a black man in a nice car. In 2020, black people are over 9.7 times more likely to be stopped and searched by police, despite being significantly less likely to be carrying drugs or arms than someone white. According to Her Majesty's Inspectorate of Constabulary and Fire & Rescue Services, and the *Guardian*, the Met Police carried out over 22,000 stop-and-searches of young black men during the coronavirus lockdown, 88 per cent of which led to no further action, which means that 19,360 black people were either physically pulled from their cars or massively inconvenienced and embarrassed for no other reason than unreasonable suspicion and stereotyping.

Ask a black man what the disappointment on a police officer's face looks like when the insurance checks out and no drugs or weapons are found in the car. Ask them if they have ever got an apology after a frisk. Ask black parents how many times they've been called into their children's school to be told that their child is in fact behaving just like the other children, but that their punishment will be ten times worse because the teachers already see them as a thug. Ask the white doctor who has suffered the majority of coronavirus deaths. Ask the black woman how many weeks she was put on the frontline with the virus without the PPE needed to protect her from it. Ask the black father who lost his black wife during pregnancy what it felt like to have their concerns ignored until it was too late. Black women are five times more likely to die in childbirth than white women in the UK. The UK Confidential Enquiry into Maternal Deaths exposed the inconsistency in responding to concerns made by black women, who were often ignored or given significantly less attention and compassion than white women in the same ward.

Ask them all how it made them feel. Ask them if they have the energy to call out the micro-aggressions that take place every single day. Ask them how much their confidence and pride in their identity has been curtailed thanks to the huge stigmas that come with their skin colour. Some of which can quite literally become a matter of life and death.

If I were to ask my white friend on the estate why he felt so comfortable talking about other black people in such a discriminatory and belittling way in front of me, I can only imagine the many ways in which he would try to convince me that he wasn't racist, with all of his excuses pointing to the very fact that I was black, and his friend, and different from the rest. Except that I didn't want to be different from the rest in order to be accepted. I wanted us all to be free of prejudice. I wanted to know that, in the same way that he helped me up from the floor one Saturday after the Chelsea Headhunter hooligans rampaged through my estate, he would help up another black child that was racially attacked. Not because they reminded him of me, but because they were a human being who deserved the same level of compassion as anyone else. I never spoke to my friend about these things. As a child, friendship was more important than racism. Or so I was forced to believe. In school it seemed like almost everything came before racism. Even the agenda of the curriculum came before the truth. It's no wonder that so many people grow up to become those police officers who feel justified in taking black lives.

From the moment are born, they are breathing in the racist misinformation from their parents, and their parents' parents, who undoubtably lived during an even more divisive era. And that is the foundation of the curriculum that our schools still teach today.

Now, before I talk about how the history of black people is packaged and studied in mainstream academia, I should begin by stating that something is better than nothing. Even if the study of black history is currently inadequate, it does at least exist today. Which is more than could be said during my own school experience.

Growing up, my study of black history was almost entirely restricted to the accent inside my elders' mouths. It was the 'Y' sound that found itself in words like 'can't'. It began and ended with my family and the stories that have created them. It built itself on the plate between the oxtail and the dumplings. My history found its voice in the reggae music that woke me and Pauline on a Saturday morning as a signal that the house would need to be cleaned any minute now. Over the years, my history predominantly disclosed itself to me in a very personal way. You can understand why this is limiting. I could tell you about my aunty and how she got her first house in London, but I could not tell you the intricate details of the Windrush generation's first few years away from home, living among people who believed they were the superior race. I could tell you about how she smiles from ear to ear whenever she sees the grandchildren, but I know little of the things that stole her joy during the sixties. I wish that, as a child, I knew why she was as protective as she was. I wish I knew the mental and physical impact of what it meant to exist as black, as a target, as a woman, as a sole provider, as a slave in the transatlantic system that uprooted and stole millions of destinies. I wish I could prescribe something to alleviate the impact of such a tragic history, but I only know as much as can be told through our experiences. And what my family do loudest is survive. My black history growing up was studying how to survive against all the odds. And that was simply not good enough, because what then can be said for the post-traumatic stress that reveals itself in anybody who has once been considered a slave? With no knowledge of who we once were, and how that all changed through the European Convention on Human Rights, how do we come to understand the disadvantages that my community is subject to today? If all we know is how to survive the system, what are we supposed to do with the micro-aggressions we experience on a day-to-day basis? Where do we go with this constant attack, when the world is adamant that we should all just get over slavery as quickly and quietly as possible?

Caribbeans who came to England to work in hospitals, build roads and operate dangerous machinery after the Second World War are still alive today. The memory of some being pulled from the home they'd known into a foreign land still lingers heavily throughout the streets of London. I can only imagine the potency of the PTSD that must sit silenced under tired tongues. The eternal 'what if?' that must plague their thoughts. The painful daydream of what their future could have been had it not been rewritten. I wonder if they ever felt the sense of 'home' here that they felt in the Caribbean. I've lived here my whole life, minus two years in Jamaica, so this is the strongest sense of home I have. Despite how patchy and painful it can be, I don't know any better. But my elders did. Just recently, our politicians were caught red-handed trying to send this generation back to the Caribbean – from the lands they were dumped on sixty years before – and in some cases succeeding. But their homeland is now as foreign to some of them as England would like to be considered all of a sudden.

The close proximity we have to the slave trade, and the impact it continues to have today, demands explanation and understanding from all races. But we need to remember that the history we are taught comes from the Western European perspective. As a wiser and older man, I've had to re-evaluate everything I've ever learnt and seek out other perspectives and then come to my own conclusions. Perhaps if we knew the truth about each other's stories and struggles, we would be slower to hate and quicker to empathise. And that is down to education.

There was a time, even when I was at school, when black history was barely taught at all. Now, in the year 2020, although black history is taught in schools, it is worth me explaining *how* it is taught. Black children are taught that their history began with slavery. Children from other ethnicities are taught that black people's story began with slavery. Slavery is taught as something that European people were able to do because they were smarter, wealthier and more powerful. When I learnt about slavery, for a moment I wondered whether this was true. I was almost embarrassed to be black. If a group of people could come and scatter one of the biggest continents in the world didn't that make them the superior race? Although this thought was only a fleeting one, some of that shame stuck with me. I don't know what the knowledge of this hostile takeover does to the ego of a white student, but it definitely leaves them more emotionally protected than the black children who have to go into the playground after the lesson. Perhaps the white children with hearts experience white guilt. But guilt is easier to digest than shame. Shame struggles to lift its melanin chin to feel deserving. Shame gets in the way of experiencing pride in your ethnicity. Shame creates a divide between those who are subjected to it, and those who will never be able to fully understand its consequences. Shame isn't resolved by the word 'sorry'. I am not a slave, and you are not a slave master, but shame doesn't know how to free itself from its bondage in many ways besides anger. After watching the graphic slavery series *Roots* as a child, I was angry. I didn't want to play out with my white friend on the estate. I didn't want to give them any more of my time. They had already taken my entire history. They had looked at me, measured my arms, hung a card with a price tag around my mother's neck, forced my sister to perform sexual acts, kidnapped me, put me on a boat, thrown my friends overboard, sold me. I knew my friend hadn't done all of this, but he benefited from the fact that it had never happened to his ancestors. And from that position of privilege, he made racist jokes. As if anything about this was the least bit funny.

In 2020, I'm not sure whether teachers should teach the whole graphic truth of the slave trade. Perhaps it is in our best interests to protect our children from how sordid a soul can become. Perhaps the anger I briefly felt after watching *Roots* would perpetuate even more rage-filled division. Look at the protest.

I do not know how helpful it is to try to cover the history of black people in two, one-hour lessons – which in some schools is all that's carved out in the curriculum to study black history. Not when the impact of it is still suffocating black people across the world. Not when the transatlantic slave trade went on for over 400 years, and no reparations were made for these centuries of displacement and captivity. Not when the history taught in the West was written by the victors. Not when the impact of a colonised curriculum is felt like a punch to the gut. Not when black children are left to doubt the historical sovereignty of blackness. And especially not if in October, during Black History Month, the only black people we are taught to celebrate are the ones who liberated black people from slavery. Our history is richer than that. Yes, the story of our diaspora is agonising, but if all that children are ever taught is that black people were slaves, and then they were free, the perception of blackness becomes one of continued weakness. Parents of black children then have the job of forcing pride into their children, since the curriculum strives to do quite the opposite, with the support of society. I find that the truth often lies between what we are taught, what we are told and what we come to discover ourselves. I've never known it to exist in its entirety in any one place. Especially not in the classroom.

I remember the relationship I had with my mother's partner, Oliver, constantly revolving around history. He is one of those men who knows a little about a lot, and lot about a little. And history was one of those things he knew a lot about. I would come home from school after a soul-destroying history lesson with a desire to be re-taught by a black man. By somebody I could listen to without feeling angry or defensive. I would learn about empires in school and develop such a curiosity about the character of dictators. What made a man do as they did? What made Oliver step in and be there for my mum all those years back when he offered to give her a lift because she was very heavily pregnant with me? What made Karl Marx reimagine the financial system? What made Hitler a murderer? I suppose, as a young boy, it was natural for me to wonder what makes a man. Especially when my own biological father only ever taught me how to disappear. Oliver would sit me down and tell me all about communism, Rasputin, Marxism, Idi Amin, Stalin, Pol Pot and everything else that I had a question about. In learning about how tainted the minds of some dictators were, I began to wonder why they were ever given such power, such a platform, such idolisation.

It's only very recently that governments across the world have begun to realise how inappropriate it is to have statues of slave owners scattered around their cities. Men who were celebrated for how many people they raped, captured and displaced. Hopefully by the time you're old enough to read this, that shocks you. But at present, believe it or not, people are arguing that statues of slavers are a part of history that needs to be preserved. It's funny, because I don't know a single person who has learnt about history from a statue. In fact, you can live underneath a statue your whole life and never read the placard at the bottom. Building an image of someone in stone or bronze is idolising what they stood for. Perhaps more than 100 years ago, it was normal to commemorate slave and plantation owners. But if we truly believed that slavery was a gross injustice in history, the statues should have become ash the moment the world learnt this. Today, you'd struggle to find a single statue of Hitler anywhere, despite his contributions to the German economy in the 1930s. His wrongdoings ensure that he is rightly villainised. I cannot understand why it's so unfathomable to extend that same treatment to other evildoers who destroyed countless innocent African lives. Surely, as an inclusive society, we aren't proud of this part of our past? Although it should be noted that our current prime minister, Boris Johnson, stated with conviction in an article in *The Spectator* in 2002 that 'The problem [with Africa] is not that we [Britain] were once in charge, but that we are not in charge any more.' He also wrote that Britain's colonial dealings with Africa were 'not a blot on our conscience'. So perhaps the resistance to removing slaver statues is rooted in that shared, sorry sentiment that black people would do well to become enslaved once again. While such notions of supremacy are still at large within our leadership, perhaps it's teachers who should take up the mantle of correcting these wayward modes of thinking.

What if, as well as talking about the slave trade, the textbooks also covered the great African kingdoms that created the very arithmetic, engineering and medicine that we study today? What if children had to study the reign of Emperor Mansa Musa while studying the great leaders that changed the world? He was a Malian sultan who lived in the fourteenth century but remains to this day the wealthiest man to ever have lived. He would raise the GDP of a town by simply walking through it with his great army, funding gold mines and farming, and creating jobs and schools for locals. What if children were taught about the gold- and oil-mining trade and irrigation systems in West Africa that fed nations across the world for years, including Europe? Perhaps if children were taught *why* the world was envious of Africa, to the point of ravaging its resources and dismantling the ancient structures that contributed to the progress of technology and health, the slavery story would be understood for the evil that it was, and the empathy that would follow would ensure a closer study of its impact on today's world. One would hope. At the very least, a wider study into the true history of our world could balance the superiority complex of the white community and empower the young black children who still suffer the consequences of slavery and perception today. Perhaps if some light was shed on the black inventors and academics that have transformed the world we live in today, it would balance things at the root. Or even encourage and inspire the young black children who otherwise grow up on stories around slavery. In the Caribbean, children are taught about people who looked just like them who went on to attend the University of the West Indies, an establishment that has been listed as a top 100 Golden Age University. It has schooled some of the brightest and brilliant minds of the 21st century. If you were to only look at Caribbean boys in the UK, and their grade averages in comparison to other ethnic groups, you'd wonder what the discrepancy really is. Because it's clearly not their capacity to study and succeed.

Black children from a Caribbean background are three and a half times more likely to be excluded from primary, secondary and special schools. Often, these exclusions take place due to a general lack of understanding and the embedded racist belief that these children are inferior or hopeless. They are excluded or given lengthy detentions for doing the exact same things that their white peers are doing – the difference being the overarching stereotype that is kept alive by the media: that black people do not know how to behave. There is also a long history of white children from working-class backgrounds being unfairly expelled and punished in schools, and a part of me wonders whether all black children are just put into the 'lower-class' grouping with other children who are there because of their family's financial position. It isn't uncommon for white children from poorer backgrounds to achieve lower grades and literacy rates than those from more affluent families. However, the prejudice faced by both groups is still very different. Although a poorer white child may be mistreated due to their class, a recent study by researchers at Princeton University, reported in the *Proceedings of the National Academy of Sciences*, has shown that while a white child will be rewarded for their confidence, a black child will be labelled as arrogant or rude. This is something experienced in the workplace, predominantly by black women, who are told that their behaviour is aggressive, despite it mirroring the tenacity of their white male colleagues, who are rewarded for their passion. The primary determiner in both of these spaces is anti-blackness.

A friend of mine has been the head teacher of two Pupil Referral Units (PRUs) – which cater for children who can't attend a mainstream school – and a teacher for around twenty-five years. During the World Cup he was part of a large teachers' group chat on WhatsApp. In the chat there were senior school governors, head teachers and other figures of authority in the education hierarchy. You would expect this group of people to be some of the most unbiased in society, given their social responsibility as educators. My friend found it to be quite the opposite. There were racist names and slurs being thrown around about the Mexican football players. And some of the black players were actually referred to as 'nig-nogs'. As much as my friend didn't want to break up the 'banter', as a black man and a teacher to some pupils who had been unfairly expelled based on their race alone, he was outraged. He messaged the chat and asked whether he was the only one who found this kind of language disgusting. He left the chat shortly after. I can only imagine what became of the chat after that. If this is how comfortable teachers are with racism behind the scenes, what hope is there for black children in the classroom, where such mindsets are suddenly empowered?

Anti-black policies have been the frequent study of educators and black scholars since the inception of mixed schools. The banning of and punishment for traditional black hairstyles such as cornrows or dreadlocks in schools is part of the subjugation of certain cultures. Cornrows are a protective style worn by both boys and girls to keep their hair healthy and in place. This is the equivalent of a white child tying their hair back in a bun. Yet only cornrows were banned from multiple schools across Britain, thus defining what was 'normal' and acceptable as that which only benefits European hair. I'm a man of optimism and would like to believe that ignorance is at the root of these oppressive decisions. So perhaps if teachers became aware of how different hair textures operate, they would come to learn that what works for white hair cannot work for Afro-Caribbean hair, and that the standard cannot be based on just one hair type. Policies like these have a huge impact on the mental wellbeing and self-confidence of children growing up, with many of them equating beauty or neatness to whiteness. This unfortunate mistruth is prevalent in many communities, from the world of bleaching in Africa, to the caste system in India, to the plastic surgery throughout the West, to the relaxing of African hair into the texture of European hair. Our unconscious internalisation of what we think of as good and bad is in desperate need of a remix.

For example, let's look at some everyday terms that carry negative connotations: Blackmail. Blacklist. Black sheep. Black mark. Black ball. Black market. And now some words that induce a sense of positivity and good-ness, enforcing the idea of whiteness as a symbol of goodness: Purity. Angel. Heaven. Jesus. Virginity. Even the term 'white lie' uses the positive attributes of the colour white to liberate the lie from its harm. What's interesting to learn is that the labels given to people's skin colour actually came after these words had been invented, meaning that 'black' and 'white' already had fixed connotations of either 'good' or 'bad' when they were attributed to people. What we must remember is that our English dictionary was first pulled together during the seventeenth century, at a time when racism was rampant and people of colour were considered inferior in every sense. So a word that already had negative connotations was attached to my skin. Imagine if a new species was discovered today and it was called 'dangerous'. What would the impact of such a title have on its existence? Just as certain offensive terms are no longer used to describe people of various religions, sexual orientations or ethnic groups, perhaps we need to take a long, hard look at the injuries that certain terms can still inflict. My skin is not black. It is not equivalent to a black hole or the night sky, something for children to be scared of. It is a specific shade of brown, more similar to the earth than a shadow. My friend's skin is not white. That is not the default colour. The Caucasian complexion is a cream colour. You may be thinking that we need these simplistic terms of black and white to describe racial groupings, but if we are grouping people based on their *race*, using the term 'human' would be much more accurate, and it would go a long way to reminding everyone that people of all colours share the exact same DNA. And if we must further define our ethnic make-up, we have the names of millions of colours to choose from that are not already injected with sub-conscious associations. We are all shades of the exact same race. I wish I didn't have to use the words 'black' and 'white' so frequently in this letter, but for now, as they are the common language that society uses, they will have to do.

Today, in 2020, 'unconscious bias' is a major buzzword. It is an academic way of saying that sometimes people do not mean to display racism, but they do it anyway because it is learnt behaviour, taught without consideration of the impact it will have on a select group. The bias that begins at a young age is then carried through into adulthood, and becomes embedded in our social infrastructure. It seems as though one of the only ways to break the cycle is to address the often-innocent root of the problem. A social experiment carried out in a South London school, which was filmed by the Channel 4 documentary *The School That Tried to End Racism* and aired in the summer of 2020, hopes to do just that. Race expert Dr Nicola Rollock helped to facilitate a social experiment on a class of eleven-year-olds in a well-performing, multicultural school in South London. The aim after three weeks of discussions and immersive un-learning was to reduce racial bias and build better children for the future. It's not uncommon for both children and adults to claim that they 'do not see colour'. In this experiment, the entry interviews with the children showed that only children from European backgrounds shared this perspective on race. The mixed-race and black children were very aware of their colour and what it meant in society. Many of them held quite celebratory views of their culture, and this was further documented once the children were asked to talk about their race in segregated groups. At this point the group of white children became very quiet and withdrawn, communicating that they felt very awkward to be grouped by their colour. This, of course, was nothing new to the children of colour who had existed in that space of 'difference' since learning they were a minority group. They then became extremely excitable, relieved to be able to speak openly about their feelings with those who shared similar experiences.

The energy of the group of white children was the polar opposite. One child very innocently stated that he would want to be defined by his fiery red hair, not knowing that he was expressing a desire to be defined by the aspect of his appearance that made him different from the rest. The luxury here, however, was that this difference does not carry with it the same prejudices and negativity that skin colour often can. To 'not see colour' is to unconsciously erase the experiences of people of colour that have occurred as a direct result of their race. Upon learning that humans share at least 99.9 per cent of the same DNA, the children became further frustrated by how race has such a huge impact on people's experiences, despite most of our biology being identical – a sentiment that I wish would flood the world.

To help inform the children about how the world is still more divided than it may seem in the playground, a final experiment was conducted. The children were asked to stand on a starting line in their PE kit, and were instructed to step backwards or forwards towards the finish line based on their responses to statements posed by their PE teacher. The children were instructed to step backwards if they ever worried about their parents being stopped and searched. They were asked to step forward if their parents had never spoken to them about the colour of their skin, and forward if English was their parents' first language. They were asked to step backwards if they were ever asked what country they came from, and backwards if they'd ever been the only person of their colour in a room. As the divide between the children widened, the game stopped being fun for them and they came to realise how impactful their colour is on the wider race of life. The positions they finished in after all of the questions had been asked were the positions they had to start from once their teacher said, 'On your marks, get set, go.' The advantage that the white students had over the children of colour became apparent, and many were moved to tears by how something as beautiful as diversity could put people at such a disadvantage.

If from a young age, before the seeds of division have had time to be watered, children could come to understand racism as something that should never be a natural response to difference, but rather as an element of society that needs major reform, perhaps we could rally troops for the fight against racism and not against each other. On the thirteenth day of the sixth month of the year, as I walked through crowds of football hooligans screaming racist chants, I was devastated to witness how ugly prejudice can become with age. Nobody is born hating somebody because of their colour. It's something we have been taught, based on a period of time when the colour of your skin determined your standing in society. Today, thanks to globalisation, we live in a melting-pot world, and the hearts and minds of our nations need to wake up to the beauty of this, instead of perpetuating our horrible, history.

CHAPTER 3

FAITH AND POLITICS

'If kindness and fairness were made a priority in everybody's hearts and minds, even if just for a moment, the world would change in a day.'

can't say that I subscribe to any one religion like most of my family, but there are a few things I do believe in. I believe that there is a higher power. One who is far too gentle and caring to resemble the men here on earth who have used religion as a tool to divide and conquer instead of unite and save. I believe that the traits I've experienced in women resemble a more God-like identity than that which I've seen in men. You may chose to agree or disagree, but one thing I think we will all have a warming understanding of, is the purity of a child's innocence. I see it in how a child gives and shares. In how they laugh and bounce light around a room. Like a child whose bright eyes are not yet tarnished by this world's misdemeanours, I truly believe that there are pockets of goodness inside every single one of us, waiting to be released and welcomed into the very DNA of our human bodies. I believe that we are built to let the light out.

Despite how suffocating our own darkness can be, a candle will always dispel that darkness, forcing it to leave our bodies and become a shadow that will become fainter and fainter, the more light we let in. It is a choice, I believe, to lean in towards the side of you that radiates goodness. It isn't always an easy choice. But the right ones can't always be easy, or we would all make them all of the time. The decision to make the better choice liberates us from our lesser selves. Our angry selves. The versions of us that feel jealousy, rage, misunderstanding or misery. These feelings are like a grip around our hearts, stopping the circulation of forgiveness, empathy and, most importantly, joy.

Joy is a form of resistance. It breaks open a tightened face and encourages it to smile. Nothing can penetrate a room like a laughing baby. Their adorable noises pierce the softest parts of us. Something that was solid becomes liquid beneath our skin and travels to meet them at their point of bliss. Have you ever watched a grandparent join in with the euphoria of a child? You must have witnessed how the decades of hardship slip from their skin, to reveal the fleshy centre of their happiness beneath. This is the joy that has always lived inside them but perhaps hasn't always been welcomed with open arms. But the arms of a child reaching out to be picked up and held … well, quite frankly there is no greater antidote to the things the world puts us through as we age. There is something about the trust that you, my children and grandchildren, have shown in me that makes me want to be a better person. I suppose that's exactly what goodness should do. It should inspire us. It should want us to crave more of it. It may not be the case when you are old enough to read this letter, but at present I try to spend as much of my time as I can with you angels. You have become essential to me. To the best version of me. When you notice that Grandad has had a tough day, and you climb onto my fatigued chest, rest your warm, chubby cheeks against my skin – the skin we share – and you tell me that you love me, I am immediately reminded of how much beauty there still is in the world.

You are able to recognise stress and know to plaster it with love, and I hope and pray that you never lose that instinct. I hope that love forever remains your first impulse. And oh, how I hope I can protect you from much of what that softness will invite. There is nothing as wise as love, but the world will spend all of its days convincing you that it's the silliest emotion of them all. Sometimes you will be convinced. Sometimes to love will feel like the stupidest thing to do. But perhaps you will remember this one thing from Grandad. From watching you grow under the loving guidance of my own children, I've learnt everything I need to learn about goodness, and everything I need to learn about the necessity of sharing love. In that, you have taught me everything I need to know about how to live properly. I hope that I am worthy of your continued efforts. There are many yet to be taught by you and by your love.

As a woman's belly grows during pregnancy, her body is stretching to double its capacity. Suddenly she eats for two. She thinks for two. She works for two. And when the baby arrives, she becomes responsible for two sets of joy, and so has to double her capacity to love. And that's after nine months of morning sickness and swollen ankles and then hours and hours of labour. I think there is a good evolutionary reason why babies are born so cute. It's entirely necessary to make it all feel worthwhile. Mum always let me know that my happiness was worth it. Even when I started growing out of my cute baby phase and into those harsh years of puberty. I remember once, towards the end of primary school, all the children were preparing for the school disco. The girls were blushing over the dresses they would get, and the boys were boasting about the designer sweatshirts they were being bought. I wanted a particular Pierre Cardin jumper so badly, and I knew it was a bit on the pricy side, but the school disco seemed like such a reasonable occasion to spend more of Mum's money on. If not now, then when? I tried to soften my face into its most adorable expression and asked Mum if she could buy me the jumper for the disco. Her lips said no, but her eyes said yes. I could tell from the melting of her stare that she hated the look of disappointment that fell over me when she explained that it was just a bit too expensive. Later on in this letter I will unpick what the real riches of life are, but this might be when I first learnt it.

My mum got me the jumper. She told me that the happiness that spread across my face was worth every last penny. Because if we cannot be led by the love we have for our loved ones' joy, to what have we given more importance?

We are all looking to be guided by love, even if we never admit it. We travel to fall in love with new food and new cultures. We meet new people to hopefully discover a unique love tucked between the time spent together. We look for jobs that will ignite a passion that justifies the amount of time we spend away from our family. We create new life with a loved one to express our love in a physical sense. We buy new things to fall in love with that have no obligation to reciprocate. We find a God. We study how that God manifests love and we try to mirror it in the hope of being loved in return, even if only by the promise of eternity. In all of these pursuits, there must be the underlying knowledge that there is a superior essence of love that exists within us, waiting to be drawn back out like a magnet. I say 'back out' because as a child we know automatically how to ensure that love explodes around our bodies like a grenade. I watch you share your toys and flood your mum with kisses, and you are so sure that what you are supposed to be is kind. I think we spend our whole lives trying to get back to that certainty, trying to stimulate the natural joyful reflex of a child. Sometimes I look at you with envy, because even in the simplest acts – just waking up, exhaling and inhaling – you have found a reason to be happy.

I suppose that's where we get it wrong as adults. Once the blissful ignorance of being a child is torn away, we begin to feel like love and goodness is something we can only find externally. At some point, happiness is reduced to something that we can only earn or buy. Sometimes it's because a bad relationship has made us feel as though someone must behave in a certain way to be deserving of kindness. Sometimes our anger towards a situation morphs into anger towards the people who caused it. And we suppress our sense of humanity due to a rage-filled decision we have made to become ruler over who deserves to live or die. Perhaps that's why equality isn't extended to black people just yet. Unfortunately, some people think we need to earn the right to stay alive, as if it isn't the birth right of all humans. Perhaps that's why some people were angry that we saved that white man's life at the protest. There was a sense that we were empowering the rhetoric that black people always have to go above and beyond, just to exist fairly. I do understand why some people were frustrated that my photo became one of the leading images of the protest. But had we let him die, how different would we really be from the people we were protesting against?

The mistake we make as adults is turning towards the wrong parts of ourselves. We think that anger and division can point us in the right direction, but it never can. It can only point us back to anger and division. And in our misguided attempts to experience some kind of resolve, we lean into these feelings instead. We incite corruption or racism – or worse, vengeance. We cannot give in to the desire for vengeance if we hope to survive as a human race. If we do not extinguish the fire in some of our feelings, we will sit in a burning world that will turn us all to ash. As I said, I do not subscribe to any particular religion, but where there is undoubtedly a higher power, it is in the moral concepts of right and wrong, where, in a dualistic world, the consequences of doing what is wrong must be equal to the act of ignoring what is right. There is always a consequence to our actions, but the saving grace is that with the gift of time comes the opportunity to grow and learn. But we must be open to learning. We must become so obsessed with what is right that change becomes an aspiration at every level of society. From the boy who doesn't want to fight any more to the politician who just wants to help people. Yes, they do exist. I am powerless to believe otherwise.

Much like my position on religion, I cannot justify aligning myself to any one particular political party. They have all taken turns to disappoint me in their own unique way. Whether through broken promises or neglect, the concerns of the communities I represent have been shown to be of little to no importance to politicians time and time again. If ever there was a news headline that summarised the dismissal of working-class and black and ethnic-minority people, it would read 'Piccaninnies, letterboxes, bestiality'. These are just a few of the labels that our leaders have used to refer to minority groups in recent years.

The Conservative Party has a long and saddening history of racism and Islamophobia and has been accused of taking on an anti-Palestinian agenda, while the Labour Party has been accused of anti-Semitism in recent years. And in a similar vein we have seen numerous deportation scandals in the last decade. In 2013, under previous Tory leadership, the then Home Secretary Theresa May headed up a 'hostile environment' strategy with the aim of making immigrants feel so unwelcome that they would

leave and 'go home'. We then saw the devastating Windrush scandal in 2018, in which British-Caribbean people who have lived here their whole lives were detained, denied benefits, threatened with deportation and in some cases illegally deported. Some were sent to a new land where they had no family, no home and no means of working. Many of these victims of illegal deportation are still trying to return home to their families in London.

According to a CNN and Savanta ComRes poll in June 2020 that surveyed British adults above the age of eighteen, 58 per cent of black Brits believe the Tory Party to be institutionally racist. During the 2019 general election campaign, it became extremely evident extremely quickly that this was surely the case. That's why the landslide vote in their favour worried me. What does that say about the true heart of Britain? As a member of the black and working-class community, it was very distressing to watch it all unfold. To see issues that were negatively impacting on my communities be supported with little resistance, while policies that would directly affect my communities were completely disregarded, was tough. For example, the Tory Party noted in their manifesto that they hoped to enforce more stop-and-search powers on the streets of London. This was proposed ahead of addressing the problems that already existed with regards to the disproportionate stop-and-searches that are carried out on black boys, which would often result in the illegal, violent handling of innocent children and teenagers. As a father, when I heard that the Tory Party hoped to extend these powers of the police, I was terrified for what that would mean for the children I raise, teach and mentor. Young black boys who seem to always fit the 'one size fits all' description of the suspect. I do wonder what is communicated on police radios ahead of a stop-and-search. I remember, whilst failing to successfully forget, an occasion in my youth, where I was stopped and searched around thirty times in one week. And no, it wasn't for any kind of bad behaviour, it was for having a new car. A Renault 5 GT Turbo. Considerably flashy at the time. A car that us boy racers loved and spent as much time as possible in.

The first time I was stopped, I was demure, polite and very calm. Yes, sir. No, sir. I collected my Producer and hoped to get on with my day undisturbed. Unfortunately, this was far too optimistic for the times I was living in. In less than thirty minutes, I was stopped again and had to go through that entire process again. Still, I remained calm and respectful. But by the third time in one day, not only was I now late to just about everything, I was furious that a black man in a nice car could be pulled over for no other reason than being a black man in a nice car. And I let the third police officer know it. I told him how ridiculous this was, and how he was the third of the day. Guess what he had the cheek to respond. He told me, 'I'll show you what stop and search really means'. I didn't think much of it at all. Usual power play. I just wanted to get on with my day. Unfortunately, I learnt quite quickly what he meant by that comment. The police officer flagged up my registration plate number on his radio, and I was stopped another six times that day. Throughout the following week or so, whenever an officer saw my car, I was stopped. Not only is this a huge, annoying inconvenience, but it's a complete exploitation of power. This was unlawful and I can't help but think that this is the kind of superiority complex that leads officers to over-exert themselves in more harmful ways.

I wonder what else was said on the radio to convince the other police officers to stop me. Maybe they said the car was carrying a weapon. Perhaps the only visible weapon they refer to in order to justify their violence is the skin colour of the victim – always on display, like a wanted poster. Black people are over-policed, and under-protected. How can we ever appear unarmed if our own skin has been weaponised?

What's worse is that this policy is not the only structural injustice for minority groups and working-class people. During the run-up to the election, there was a lack of conversation around legal aid and how necessary it is if those from disadvantaged backgrounds are going to continue to be unfairly accused of crimes. Lawyers are an expense that most working-class families can't afford. Imagine being an innocent victim of arrest, and not having the means to fight your case. In a documentary I watched on Netflix called *13th*, film-maker Ava DuVernay exposes that 97 per cent of the prison population in America are there for no other reason than because they could not afford to go through a trial. In the UK we have a similar system that will treat you better if you are guilty, rich and white than if you are poor and innocent. Millions of innocent people across the world are sitting in prison today for no other reason than their financial standing. How is that justice? The Tory Party did not comment on this during the election campaign, despite justice being the bedrock of a fair society. Perhaps it is because these issues do not traditionally implicate their voting demographic.

In 2019, the Labour Party took 64 per cent of the black vote. Over the years, the Labour Party has been considered 'the black party'. And let's face it, Labour has always had a more inclusive vision for Britain, caring considerably more for the working-class population than any other party. Sometimes I vote for Labour because I cannot stand with the Tory manifesto. My mother voted Labour because they pushed for workers' rights and a welfare state. Her mother before her may have voted Labour for those exact same reasons. And although I do not agree with everything that Corbyn stands for, sometimes you have to vote for the lesser of two evils in that moment. Unfortunately, there is no perfect party. And now I know that the working-class and black or minority groups do not share one homogeneous perspective on every issue. That is why 20 per cent of us voted for the Tories in 2019. But I do believe that if we come together as a community to consolidate our votes and make it clear that politicians have to earn our collective voting power, then at the very least our more mutual problems will be addressed.

All of that being said, over the years, my faith in politics has been shattered. Look at the very reason why you are reading this letter: because a group of people wanted to validate the police's killing of black people, and I had to take to the streets to perform the role of the law enforcers. If ever there was a postcard for 2020, I'm sure that viral photograph of me largely fits the bill. Not because I'm a hero, but because it acts as a visual representation of what we are still having to do in the twenty-first century. I'll keep on saying it: I had no plan to become a national hero or a spokesperson for equality. But what I will say is something that has been said before. I saw it on a poster of Morgan Freeman, although I don't think he said it himself; I think it's from his 2007 film *Evan Almighty*. Either way, it read: 'How do we change the world? One random act of kindness at a time.'

I wholeheartedly agree. If one smile from a baby can lift an unsuspecting passer-by's mood for the day, if somebody offering you a seat on the train can alleviate the day's stresses, if a selfless act of kindness can inspire that same kindness to flow from you into somebody else, then as humans we have the power to ignite a beautiful butterfly effect. If kindness and fairness were made a priority in everybody's hearts and minds, even if just for a moment, the world would change in a day.

* * *

At the age of forty, I had this exact revelation while I was sitting at a desk in the City of London, crunching data for a big bank. I was twenty-five years deep into my role in IT, and towards the final few years I could feel the relationship I had with this career breaking down. This turned out to be reciprocal, because after four years at my last company in the City, my contract was not renewed. The job and I no longer served each other as we used to. I had initially got into the field of computer science and finance after having my first son at nineteen. I realised then that graduating from university was no longer an option, and that I needed to start earning some real money to be able to provide the life for my child that my own father did not even attempt to provide for me. I got my first job in the City, and the pay cheque at the end of the month kept me there for almost three decades. That, coupled with the desire to love and support my children in every possible way.

However, the voice in my heart had started to become louder than the voice in my pocket. It seemed as though the part of me that knew I was put here to help others was waiting for the perfect time to explode. My mum had always tried to push me down the route of education, and I know that one of the main reasons she did this was because she was not able to pursue her own studies. Her life had had to revolve around her family almost as soon as she became part of one. My mother is the kind of woman who would take the skin off her own back to keep her children warm. In fact, in many ways, that's exactly what she did when Pauline and I were young. She would sometimes work late into the evenings but would still have dinner, a packed lunch and a healthy breakfast prepared for us. Growing up, I could physically feel the love that oozed from the women in my life. The level of compassion that they displayed sank deep into my DNA and eventually broke out in a complete career change. I knew that I needed to extend my parenting instinct beyond my own children and scatter this love more widely through the medium of sport.

I had finally realised that I was put here to serve. To extract the better parts of people. Some might say that's because I possess the typical traits of a Libra, which is most evident in my pursuit of balance and fairness. I believe in hearing both sides of the story in any situation, and in making a just decision relative to the context. This all filtered down and found a purpose in my second career as a personal trainer. Watching somebody become empowered by realising their own potential is like a drug to me – the only drug I need to keep doing what I do. To build up somebody's body is to build up their self-belief. And to do that is to build up their confidence, which is crucial for accepting one's own flaws and feeling ready to invite necessary change. Change is something we need in our community. On so many levels, the neglect can be quantified. The general health of an area is a huge tell on its depravity. According to the National Child Measurement Programme publication for 2018/19, '[in] children living in the most deprived areas, obesity prevalence was more than double that of those living in the least deprived areas, for both Reception and Year 6'. What saddens me is the cycle it then creates – the eating habits that are passed down from the chicken and alcohol shops to the children to their own children. I feel obligated to inject this cycle with sport. With knowledge on health and fitness. Because that doesn't only change our body, it changes our story.

Through martial arts, I've found this to be true time and time again. In equipping people, mostly young men, with the skills to control their power, channel their strength and improve their focus, I've watched boys become the most admirable young men within the walls of our gym. I've witnessed anger convert into understanding and forgiveness. I've seen boys come in who are subconsciously searching for a father figure to guide them through life, and I cannot begin to express how grateful I am to be able to step into that role for so many young people. The job may not offer as much financial remuneration as IT, but instead the wealth comes from living a wholesome life of service. Although my mum has always been the closest example of perfection to me, there are some things that a woman cannot teach a boy – and there are some things that *only* a mother can teach a boy. I became a product of fatherlessness, and I've watched my son Dominic become a product of motherlessness. From the age of six, he did not live with his mum; he stayed with me. Although my mother, my sister Pauline, Aunty Toni and I all tried our best to fill that void of Dominic not having his mother around, the love that only a mother can provide has eluded him. I am most proud of him because of the difficulties he has faced and how he has come out the other side now as a single father himself, raising his four-year-old daughter, Asia. He's done a better job than I might have, had the void that my father left not been filled with something that fitted almost perfectly. Almost. In a barber shop one day I discovered I had brothers, and this undoubtedly improved my childhood. But I'll tell you that story a little later on.

CHAPTER 4

THE FABRIC OF A BLACK MAN

'We dare to hope. To dream. To believe in better.
Blind faith is a form of resistance.'

Children and grandchildren, another thing we all have in common: in this present moment, wherever we are in the world, we are made up of everything that has ever happened to us. Every lesson we have ever been taught. Every conversation, every argument we have had. Every single thing that love and hate has grown in us.

Everything we've been told and everything we've ever felt is printed on the painting that is our character. We are made up of the time between every breath we have ever taken. What we see with our eyes impacts on the lens through which we look upon life. What we hear seasons the lips from which we speak. What we read inscribes itself on our thought processes like a toddler with a fist full of crayons in a room of white walls. We live inside the room of our experiences. It is human nature to see and believe only as far as we can experience or explain. We find comfort in the glass ceiling of our thoughts and hopes. But these limitations can never work in unison with the rate of growth that we also desire as people whose essence is to transform, whether we are talking about the very primitive act of growing teeth, growing hair, growing skin cells, growing in height and build. Or whether we are talking about the transformations that we obligate ourselves to in tandem with time. Growing in knowledge. In experiences. In perspectives. As our years stretch, our understanding of things stretches with it.

So we give thanks for textbooks. We give thanks for art. We give thanks for artefacts. We give thanks for ancient preservation methods and camera phones. For poets and essayist. For visionaries and creatives. And for mothers, who will always believe in better for their children. Sometimes even better than the furthest part of their imagination. I call this blind faith. And I truly believe that we all survive vicariously through it. We put our hope in a balanced world, despite our world filling us with division and inequality on every level. No man has seen, no book has told, of a time in which the world was not at war with itself. Yet we dare to hope. To dream. To believe in better. Blind faith is a form of resistance. It works against everything we have learnt in history lessons. It works against the news channels that remind us of what this planet is filled with.

Blind faith works against our own experiences. But of all the things I am hopeful about, I am most hopeful that blind faith can work. To stop believing in this, even for a second, is to die to tomorrow.

When the American physicist Shirley Jackson sent off her application to complete a PhD in nuclear physics at MIT in the late 1960s, she was of the belief that, with time and research, she could contribute to the revolution of telecommunications that would take off in the seventies. While the rest of America marvelled at their thigh-sized cell phones, Shirley Jackson looked at the phone and asked herself: 'I wonder whether we can create a screen that allows us to touch it, without pushing down on buttons?' It had never been done. This was an activation of blind faith. Another thing that had never been done was enrolling a black woman onto a PhD course at MIT, one of the world's most prestigious educational institutes. Again, Ms Jackson allowed blind faith to chisel through every glass ceiling that the world had built in her mind, and she enrolled – making a crack in history in the process and leaving a staircase-shaped scar along the body of MIT for other black women to follow. Thanks to her imagination, intelligence and blind faith, today we have touchscreen phones. In fact, judging by the number of things I find scattered around the house after all my nieces and nephews have been over, we have touchscreen everything. Shirley Jackson owns part of our future and part of our thanks.

Blind faith changes the world. It adds a new angle to our perspective. The promise of our potential pushes each generation and civilisation forwards. Oil painting used to be an activity done only by those who could afford to spend the entire day in an art studio. This was because the oil paint would dry up so quickly that paintings had to be done in one sitting, unless the painter could afford to buy new paints each time they sat down to create. One day in the 1840s, John G. Rand woke up and realised that what the art world needed was some

way of preserving the oil paints. He plunged into his imagination and pulled out the concept of zinc tubes that would preserve and protect the texture of oil paint. Today, because of that man's forward thinking, art has become an accessible line of work and play. The healing properties of painting therapy can now be experienced by those who most need it. Rand's moment of manifesting his imagination went on to save lives. In fact, via the very act of releasing somebody's tension through painting, he has allowed them to see a world beyond their stress. To reimagine a world that isn't bogged down with anxiety or anger. Thanks to those who are brave enough to action their imagination, the world has changed time and time again for the better.

This is why we must protect our activists. Because they have envisioned a future that will better serve a diverse world. And unless we want to be protesting against the same old problems 100 years from now, we need to break the cycle by listening. By learning. By filling ourselves with new perspectives and news ways of thinking.

I am a sports fan. I was an NFL fan. But now I'm just a Colin Kaepernick fan. When others could not, he saw how impactful activism could be in the midst of the National Football League – an alliance that has brought in some of the most patriotic Americans that the continent has to offer. While most sportsmen in this space would prefer to keep their heads down and play a good game, Kaepernick saw the impact that a statement made in this particular arena could have on the conversations surrounding race and brutality. Although the world in which we live today has massively improved over the years with regards to race, the need to keep repeating ourselves does make me wonder how long we will be protesting for. I wonder how many protests we will need to fill the world with before people finally dust off old perspectives and embrace the luxury of diversity. Racism has existed in America for as long as the national anthem has been sung. Especially in sport. It's quite unbelievable when you break it down. People pay good money to come and supposedly support somebody, only to refuse that person's right to equality at the same time. They sit in the stands and hurl racist abuse at the players who contribute to the sport they know and love – something that we see much of in English football, too. That cognitive dissonance in separating the person from the passion is worrying. That ability to see them as workers who serve their own interest, without ever extending an ounce of concern towards their survival or peace. I might be wrong for saying it, but doesn't that mindset resemble something we've seen before? In the cotton fields and the servants' quarters of the wealthy? But I digress. During the national anthem before the pre-season games in 2016, Colin Kaepernick refused to stand and later took a knee. In the press conference that followed, he explained that he was 'not going to stand up to show pride in a flag for a country that oppresses black people and people of colour. To me, this is bigger than football, and it would be selfish on my part to look the other way. There are bodies in the street and people getting paid leave and getting away with murder.' It should be noted that in 2020, 70 per cent of NFL players are black. Once this statement had been made, more people were able to empathise with his actions. It made both logical and emotional sense to show solidarity with the cause that was killing so many black people just like Colin Kaepernick and 70 per cent of the entire league. However, as I said at the start of this letter, sometimes there is a glass ceiling that stops people from exploring a new perspective. The NFL was furious with Kaepernick, as well as the other players who had begun to understand and join in with his protest. I was so disappointed to see how the sport turned its back on him. Although some fans, players and even huge companies such as Nike endorsed and supported him, the very NFL that flourishes on the backs of black men refused to consider the impact of police brutality on their own players. Joe Lockhart, the former NFL vice president of communications in 2016–18, said that re-signing Kaepernick was 'bad for business'. Donald

Trump agreed and told the press that NFL owners should begin firing players who did what Kaepernick so bravely did.

Kaepernick joins a long line of athletes who have used their platform to expose injustice and call for action. He shares the same vision and blind faith that was present in Muhammad Ali, Tommie Smith, John Carlos, Billie Jean

King and many others. Although not everybody was convinced by these athletes' actions, enough heads were turned to further the conversations that can challenge people's perspective. Sport has always been good for that. If you are of the opinion that women are weak and then you watch a women's mixed martial arts fight, you should leave with a new page added to your book of perception. It should shape your thinking to support the idea that women are not weak or fragile. They can train and fight and break blocks of wood with their bare hands just as men can. Watching fighting in the movies growing up birthed an entirely new chapter in my head. This is why art is important. It's pivotal for stretching the imagination. I would watch kung fu films with my mum and sister, making a note of the moves and manoeuvres I loved. I would try to copy them after the film had finished, creating carnage at home. In my head, I was a fighter. Luckily I found a safer outlet for this on the mat in a taekwondo gym at the age of thirteen.

Like most boys, I loved sport and fitness growing up. Unlike most young boys who go on to become professional athletes, I had to look after my little sister when my mum was at work in the evenings. I do wonder what I could have become if I'd been given the opportunity to delve deeper into sport as a child. I guess there isn't a grandad alive who isn't sure he could've made the big leagues if it weren't for one thing or another preventing him from fulfilling his destiny. Perhaps that lack of activity early on is what has fuelled my interest in sport and fitness today. Not just for me, but for my two little girls. Sidéna and Kendal are enrolled in dance classes, gymnastics, swimming, football and martial arts. We keep them busy, we keep them driven and we keep them healthy. I try to do the same for myself.

Things on the sports side are a bit slower at the moment, as my calendar has had to do a complete 360 since the protests. But before radio and television and this letter came along, I would travel to Thailand and train in some of the toughest training camps around.

Although some of my *Krus* (instructors) have competed out there and tried to have me fight out there, I haven't had the chance yet. When or if things ever calm down again, I'd love to continue fighting and to delve deeper into Brazilian jiu-jitsu. I'm a blue belt red tag in taekwondo, but I do a lot of Muay Thai, or Thai boxing, too. This type of fighting has changed and maybe saved my life in more ways than can be identified. In a world of mental illness, racism and stress, sport helps me stay sane. It releases endorphins and focuses my mind on my body, my health and my skills. I do believe that sports should be an essential part of everyone's life. It has been proven time and time again to alleviate stress, reduce anxiety and transform people's moods. Not to mention the fact that it improves people's physical appearance, which contributes to a person's confidence. Going back to how I started this letter, talking about the things that create us … sport creates me. The discipline I've learnt from fitness has carried me through life. The level of accuracy I've had to acquire being a man of my size with my power has surely contributed to how delicate I am with you, my daughters and grandchildren. I might be a fighter on the mat – careful and skilled, but powerful – but I try to only bring the care home.

Being intentional is such a large part of my personality. Everything in life has demanded that of me – most of all, my family. Having lived in my own body for around fifty years, it's a wonder why some corners of the world can only see a threat when they see me. I lift my little girls onto my neck or take their hands and walk through the park. But somehow I still look like a weapon to so many. I guess this is where perception comes in again. Perception is a funny little thing. In a split second, with a passing comment or a provocative headline, something you would never have assumed about a person becomes fact in your mind's eye. And for this perception to change it must be replaced with something else. The more that perception is supported, validated and perpetuated, the harder it becomes to change and the more cemented it becomes in your belief system. Until one day the scaffolding is cleared and you live in the house of that opinion, with no recollection of how it was built within you. I think that's how some people's perception of black men became fact in their head. Somebody somewhere said that black men are aggressive, and with that seed planted in a head of a person who has never built a relationship with a black man, the world begins to water it. That person turns on MTV and sees gangster rappers talking about the hoods they grew up in, and that seed becomes a small seedling. They switch to the news and the headline is reporting a black man fighting a policeman. The seedling grows a little taller. They open a textbook and see that civil rights activists have burnt down a police station and the plant begins to bud. Soon enough, society has watered that initial seed into a flower that sits in the garden of that person's mind. Now, the flower can of course be uprooted, but the information to do so isn't accessible to that gardener. What they do not know about the gangster rapper who talks about his hood is that the housing system works against black people. It's twice as likely for a black person to be denied a mortgage than a white person with a similar credit history. This real-estate bias exists at every stage of buying a house, impacting on where you can buy and what you can buy. This has meant that many black families earning the national average wage find themselves buying houses in less affluent areas, which are habitually neglected by their local MPs. Deprived children in these working-class areas are often found to be bored following the closure of hundreds of youth clubs and parks, and these are the very conditions that breed crime in any society. That's evident in all ethnic groups. So when the rapper talks about his hood, he is documenting his own experiences, which have been built on the foundations of unequal wealth distribution. I would probably be angry in my lyrics, too.

Another thing the gardener is unaware of is that the black man who was caught on camera attacking the police officer was terrified for his life, because he has seen how easily police officers kill black people. This man has a family at home. He cannot afford to keep his hands to himself and potentially be killed for the sake of complicity.

The gardener has also missed the reason for the burning down of police stations during the protest. To her, it's a mindless act of anarchy, but she doesn't understand that this tension between the police and black people has been building and breaking for years across the world. Their textbooks have neglected to say that policemen during the Jim Crow era were raping young black women. They were robbing girls of their innocence and laughing about it over lunch. As a father of four and grandfather of four,

I do not even want to think about how I would react if the women in question were my angels.

See, the thing about perception is that it can be built on half-truths and somehow still grow into a full-sized tree. Especially when it comes to race and the far-right agenda to further racial tensions.

I believe that if this gardener were to sit down for a second, ignore their garden, read the other side of the story and spend some time getting to know a black man for the strong and loving man that he is, that garden of fear would be cut down. It might not happen straight away, but that's why the effort to show the other side of the black man and the black family is so crucial to this world's unlearning. For example, I loved watching *The Fresh Prince of Bel Air*. It showed a strong, successful black family doing the typical black-family things that rarely ever get shown – or at least not as often as the broken images of blackness. The show reminded me of my own family. I take my girls on outings. We have movie nights. We hold family picnics where the laughter could vibrate the whole of South London into a smile. The love runs deep in my family. As is the case for most black families. That love just isn't ever shown with the same enthusiasm as our trials.

Every racial group has their problems. Correction: every human alive has their problems. It is irresponsible to only ever highlight the negative side of a culture, and straight-up dangerous to inflate it into something way bigger than it actually is. I've seen how stereotypes can reduce a person's confidence and character. I can't tell you how many times I've heard that black women are aggressive in reference to behaviour that looks exactly like a white man's, who will instead be called passionate. I love black women. I love how driven they are. How passionate and compassionate they are. I love that they have laughs that can turn heads and bodies that can break necks. It's genuinely upsetting to think that someone will look at my daughters or their mothers and instantly write them off as aggressive or rude. If only the world knew that angels walk among us in the form of black mothers and daughters. I feel entirely duty-bound to shower my children with love, because I know the world might try to suppress elements of their character at one point or another. In fact, I'm sure my children's mums will tell you that I am so focused on my angels that I forget how to distribute the love evenly. Sometimes I even forget what it means to love myself. But if this is at the cost of giving my children the attention they deserve, I have no regrets. They come first every single time, just as Pauline and I came first to my mother, and you, Asia, Kyrie and Theo, have always come first to my children, Dominic and Tyler.

CHAPTER 5

OCCUPATION VERSUS EMPLOYMENT

'I hope passion finds you early on and carries you into its future.'

'*Because I said so.*'

Put that on a T-shirt and give it to all the children of the diaspora. Let them wear the words of their parents. They might be South Asian, sulking on their way upstairs to bury their head in a chemistry textbook aimed at sixteen-year-olds. At thirteen years old, they just cannot understand why their parents are so insistent on them memorising the periodic table. The child might be African, closing the tabs on his laptop screen on his preferred university degree in creative writing or music, only to end up applying to various law and engineering degrees at Russell Group universities instead. And why? Why are there thousands of children burying their heads in their hands? Hands that look just like their parents' but itch to do so much more than their parents can even envision. Why?

'*Because I said so.*'

A preferred parenting style of the survivalist genera-tion. I call them the survivalist parents because their relationship with work is based purely on staying alive and stable. For many of them, they came into the UK at a time when they did not have the luxury of aligning work with a passion. The idea of a career was not synon-ymous with pursuing an interest or fulfilling a purpose. In fact, purpose was strongly linked to making money, and often, for the parents of the diaspora, the prospect of making money is restricted to a few professions. They visit hospitals, so they are aware of doctors and how much they can earn. They use banks, so they are aware of the financial sector and how much money can be made there. They need lawyers and see them in their shiny suits. These are some of the few professions that parents from the diaspora can see their children making a living from. It's ironic, really, because they also see musicians. They see artists and small business owners. They wear clothes made by designers and consume tele-vision shows filled with actors. They save money to visit the theatre and look forward to a weekend of live perfor-mance. But somehow, these professions are rarely encouraged in the lives of their own children. I can spend time writing down my many guesses as to why this might be the case, but I'm sure that for every family it differs.

I'm sure that a father somewhere is pushing his son into law because his own parents had a tough time with their immigration or visa application and suffered the consequences. Somewhere a child is struggling to understand why her mum has pulled her from performing arts school on the weekends and instead filled her Saturday afternoons with piano playing or maths tutoring. What the young lady does not know is that her mum once read an article on what it was like being a woman in show business. She read about inappropriate directors and the troubling casting process, which often resulted in nudity or underage drinking. For one reason or another, parents from a generation that didn't have the luxury of living in service to their passion nudge their children in the direction of careers that they think will be most suitable and sustainable.

Sometimes suitability isn't even based on fears around certain industries. Sometimes the concept of suitability is built around the communities they exist in. Some parents love to be able say that their child graduated from a top university and now practises dentistry. Some parents do not come from a society that celebrates children becoming dancers. This has always amused me because, especially in African, South Asian and Caribbean communities, if there's one thing we all have in common, it's our love of dance and the arts.

The optimist in me would like to think that if a parent was to deter their child from a hobby, it would be for reasons grounded in love. That love resting in the memory of how hard it can be to live and enjoy life while struggling financially. For the black community in the eighties and nineties, this memory was very much being lived. My mother woke up at 4 a.m. to do a morning cleaning job and then came home to get us ready for school before going out again to work. I'm sure she would have loved to spend all of her evenings sitting in front of the television watching kung fu films with Pauline and me. I'm sure Pauline would have hated watching those movies on a loop, but given my mother's interest in them when I was the only one in the house who really loved them, I would like to think that she would have loved to spend more time with us watching action movies. Even if it was only for the opportunity to engage in my own joy.

It's funny, the line that is drawn between enjoying your child's joy and protecting their joy by redirecting it away from their hobbies. In parenting, if there is one thing I have learnt, four children on, is that two things can be true at the very same time. I know that my mother was as in love with our happiness as she was with life. I'm sure the two existed within each other. She sent me to a football club and she sent me to school. But by necessity, which is the essence of the working classes, at some stage she had to decide which would become a priority. The other day she revealed why she made the decision that she did on my behalf, with little say from me. She looked to the future and learnt that IT and computers were about to take over the world. She looked at my classmates and saw how many black children were being pushed into sports as the only option to succeed in life. She said the decision was easy.

My mum knew that more and more opportunities would open up in the world of computers, and that left a wider window for her son to be a part of that revolution. Now that I write this down, I'm actually quite impressed by her foresight. I don't know how many parents today would get their children an iPhone and encourage them to become influencers, despite it being one of the fastest-growing industries in the world. I suppose Mum was a visionary. Perhaps she also envisioned me having my son at the age of nineteen. Which, funnily enough, is not the most unusual thing to happen to young professional footballers. I'm sure there are more young fathers in football than IT. I suppose life starts at the pace of your pocket sometimes, and they make a lot of money quite early on. Either way, I became an IT infrastructure professional soon after becoming a dad. I had to. And I remained one for twenty-three years. I thought I had to do that, too. Mum enjoyed watching the established route play out.

Especially since my sister Pauline had done quite the opposite.

Despite my mum's best efforts to de-incentivise her from the less proven route, my sister pursued fashion design and textiles. She would spend her days at the sewing machine, patching, pinching, pinning and pruning her creations in the hope of becoming the next Vera Wang. As a child, you inhale this very simple approach to life. 'I like what this person does, I can do it, too.' So we see the footballers with the cars, and the designers with the fancy shops. We see the CEOs with holiday homes in Malibu. We see it and we decide that we want it. But only the lucky few acquire it.

Motivational speakers will tell you that you can achieve it all. That it can all be yours if you wake up at 5 a.m., change your friendship group and go vegan. What they fail to account for is generational wealth, structural discrimination and a world of glass ceilings that bounce the reflection of working-class faces right back onto their hopeful cheeks. My sister saw Nike. She envisioned Vera Wang. She didn't, however, have the bank of Mum and Dad at her disposal like most of the biggest fashion designers today. She didn't have a network of aunts and uncles that had been building careers in the UK for the past ninety years. What she had was a sewing machine, a course at Westminster and then Croydon College and some dresses and red-carpet dreams. Perhaps if my mum was able to pay to send her to a specialised school or extra curricular class from a young age, opportunity would have met her halfway. But the unfortunate reality for a lot of working-class children is that the main thing standing between them and their dream job is a parent who is only just about making the mortgage payments every month.

You may read this and immediately think of 100 examples of working-class success stories, from Joyce Meyer to Jay-Z, but the statistics really speak for themselves. It's proven that children who are able to participate in extra-curricular activities do better in life than those who are unable due to lack of resources, whether that resource is money or the youth clubs that have closed down in London today. I'll paint a picture based on a report I've just read. I'll change the names and locations, but the general gist will be as reported in a study from Brown University's Annenberg Institute for School Reform. So …

What we have here is a classic case of two very different tales from the exact same city. I'm choosing to base this scenario in the city of London. In the borough of Kensington and Chelsea. For those of you who may not be familiar with this borough, it became the poster child for financial discrepancies in 2017 following the tragic fire at Grenfell Tower. Some of the wealthiest people in London live in this borough, and so do some of the poorest. Jamie lives in the nicer part. In a private, gated community near its own set of stores and churches. He is in his first year of studies at the University of Oxford. His family have always been defined as middle class and he has enjoyed extra-curricular activities his entire life. He played football, he learnt to play musical instruments, he joined an athletics team and became a Boy Scout at an early age. His parents would swap out video games and dinner by the television for hiking trips across England, where he would learn to start fires, pitch tents and identify different kinds of birds and plants. Jamie's dad would also volunteer from time to time with his school sports team (this means that he not only had the time to take on more work, but he had the money to do it for free).

Jamie's mum was more interested in raising an integrated English child. She helped him register to vote at eighteen and remained invested in his homework and friendship groups.

A ten-minute drive down the road, we meet Kerry. She lives in the same borough but in high-rise council housing with dangerous cladding. Kerry's estate is so dangerous that she was never allowed to play outside or visit friends when she was little. While her parents took turns to work night shifts to keep food on the table, Kerry spent most of her time in front of the TV. The only lives she was internalising were her own, the crime-ridden lives of those around her and the ones she would see on TV. When she joined her high school, she identified with the children she had seen on TV who misbehaved and looked like the ones from her estate, so she emulated their behaviour. Her circle of influence did not expand, it just perpetuated itself. She began smoking weed and missing lessons with her new friends. In an attempt to pursue something better she joined a dance class. The costumes and travel to competitions cost almost £1,000 annually so she had to drop out after a year. It was not a cost that could be prioritised above three meals a day and a roof over the family's head.

Kerry then became pregnant with a man who turned out to be abusive. Today she is a single mother at nineteen who works in a kitchen that pays just enough to cover food, nappies and some clothes from charity shops. She has just borrowed £10,000 to pay for a qualification of sorts, but where that could lead to is not certain.

Although the names and locations have been changed, these are both true stories. The report goes on to conclude that:

This disparity exacerbates the already-growing income achievement gap that has kept poor children behind in school and later in life. While upper- and middle-class students have become more active in school clubs and sports teams over the past four decades, their working-class peers have become increasingly disengaged and disconnected, particularly since their participation rates started plummeting in the nineties.

Extra-curricular sporting activities transformed my life. I can say this free of exaggeration. My football team contributed to almost every aspect of my upbringing. I have no idea what I would be like if it wasn't for Stormont AFC. I'm not saying that I was made for football and it was made for me. Although I'm sure that if I had known at the time that it takes ten thousand hours of practice to become an expert at something, I would have been doing kick-ups in front of our maisonette every single day, even while babysitting Pauline – another activity that made me appreciate the time I spent with my teammates even more.

My friends and I set up Stormont AFC in 1997 in our late twenties, stemming from the youth club we all used to attend. I'm still really good friends with most of them. Trevor Edward, Darren Goodman, Fabian Ashuan, Paul Allen (who doubles as my cousin), Patrick Amponsah and Michael Augustine. We were the founding fathers of our great team and we named ourselves after Stormont Road in Battersea. It ran for around five seasons. We were big time – in our eyes anyway. We won a few cups, including the League Cup in 2000/2001. I've actually had this cup in my house for twenty years. If any of the players are reading this, feel free to come and take it off me.

I'm not even sure that I was good enough to be the one holding onto the trophy for this long. I was very average at football, but my one claim to footballing fame was playing for Heathbrook football team in my teenage years and being on the same side as Jamie Lawrence and Frank Sinclair, who both went on to become highly decorated professional footballers, reaching the highest echelons of the sport. Frank had the highest leap and did the best header of a ball I'd ever seen as a boy and was also super-fast on his feet. Jamie was the most skilful player I'd ever seen in that age group; he would take on a whole team and score. I even saw him score from corners on more than one occasion. Funnily enough, he has written his own book called *From Prison to the Premiership* – if that's not an inspirational story, I don't know what is.

But back to Stormont. The League Cup doesn't mean so much to me because we won; its sentiment is in the memories I have of training and playing with my friends. My brothers. There is something about sweating, studying, fighting sometimes, losing and winning with a group of people that creates a strong bond. I'd be excited every Sunday to get to Clapham Common and kick on the boots, crank up the bants and kick a ball for a few hours. It was such a fun period of my life.

The joy softened me, while the rawness of a group of young men together calloused my skin. There was all the usual banter, but I didn't get teased that much. Maybe it was the weight training I did. I do remember the jokes I participated in though. Trevor Edward was our top scorer. A brilliant one at that. But once we had seen him in a few games, he earnt the tag name 'Jigsaw'. The man used to fall to pieces in the box. It's a wonder how he scored so many goals because I have so many memories of him missing such easy sitters. Sitters are what we call obvious goals. And obvious goals were Trevor's kryptonite. Football, or perhaps the brotherhood of the team that is still strong today, is ingrained into my DNA.

When Labour was in power, they understood that a welfare state was essential if we wanted to create a level playing field and equal opportunities for everyone. Unfortunately, this vision left when the party did. Since then we have seen the closing down of youth clubs in working-class areas that are predominantly African, Caribbean and Asian. The families that need a free place for their children to develop and interact more than any other minority group.

I didn't plan to write a lesson about the activity gap, but I do think this explains why my sister Pauline didn't get to action her passion it its entirety. She ended up having to let that dream go and get a job as a part-time care assistant in hospital in Barnes whilst continuing her studies and working another job in a forensic mental health unit on Landore Road. Pauline had to swap her vision of tending to runway models for caring for the elderly with severe dementia and supporting criminals with severe mental health issues. She didn't have a financial safety net safe enough to pursue her original design dreams.

Pauline quickly decided that she couldn't work in the care home forever. We definitely share the same blood. Led by her growing interest in her part-time job working with criminals, she quickly realised that she had a real interest in criminology and rehabilitation. She went back to university and picked up two degrees. One in Social Policy from Roehampton Institute, and the second in Criminal Justice from Hertfordshire University. Today she puts her intelligence to good use as a probation officer and I believe that she is happy. At least I hope so. The feeling of finally finding happiness in a job that you have to wake up and do every morning is truly underrated. I wish this feeling on every single human under the sun. I hope you do not have to wait as long as I did to experience this. I hope you find and follow the things that bring you joy. I'd like to think society would still be able function if everyone did what they had a passion for. Perhaps not. But it is still vital to encourage the journey into one's purpose, at the very least. You never know what you might find.

I worked in the City for twenty-three years. I started in operations and finished in project management. I never saw this as an occupation, just as a means to an end. Something that I had to do to earn money to support my new family. Could I say I ever enjoyed it? I'm not sure, to be honest. I don't think I saw work as something I was meant to enjoy. That said, I'm sure it wasn't meant to become something I resented as much as I did. I did not enjoy the culture of working in the City. The competition was suffocating, the racism was subtle but penetrating, and the lifestyle was deadly. Quite literally. The number of suicides that happen in the City is terrifying.

There was something about waking up every morning and going to greet a manager who clearly did not like me that made the whole week very tough. People from black communities can experience racism in their personal lives that ranges from casual jokes to explicit hurtful comments and verbal or physical aggression. Surely that's why the risk of psychosis in black Caribbean groups is estimated to be nearly seven times higher than that in the white population.

When I worked at a Dutch investment bank, I had a manager who would make his disdain for me and my Asian colleague very evident. Over the years I developed a talent for sniffing out characters that might become contentious further down the line. I'd pick up on those who avoided eye contact. Who always laughed at the wrong jokes. Who would interrupt me as I spoke. Who would pass comments on my work. Who would make black jokes. I guess this is something we all do for different reasons. A woman might quickly suss out which of her male colleagues is sexist and which is trying to move to her. My Nancy Drew skill was reserved for race. Who had a problem with black people? He did. This manager of mine would find fault in my work where there was no fault. I'd ask other managers to double check things and they would always tell me that it was correct.

You might think this was a petty work drama, but it filtered into my salary. And there should be nothing petty about a pay cheque. Although we weren't encouraged to discuss our salaries in the office, we did anyway. This is how I discovered that I was getting paid less than colleagues who did the same job as me. I later found out that on average black men don't consider negotiating their salaries due to being made to feel 'lucky to be there'. This is one problem with affirmative action in the workplace. But I wasn't there to fulfil a quota. Once I learnt this, I knew I had to demand a pay rise. Especially since I was coming in every day and enduring this hostile manager. There was no way I was about to put up with being underpaid as well.

I took the matter to HR and I got my pay rise. One thing I learnt in the City is that when the system works against you, for whatever reason, sometimes you have to take matters into your own hands. Now, I couldn't control the fact that in my twenty-three years there I only ever knew of two black senior managers and one Asian. I couldn't control that there were no black faces in the boardrooms at the time. But what was within my control was ensuring that I was paid correctly and respected in the office. There was this one guy who loved to make me the butt of a joke. He would find a reason to laugh at me every opportunity he got. And on one fine Tuesday morning, I'd had it. I figured that since I'd never take such attitude outside of the office, there was no reason to tolerate it in the office, where I spent most of my life. So one day I said to the fella that life exists outside of the office, and I'd be more than happy to have the conversation outside of the walls that seemed to protect him. He never made a joke again. Bullying of any kind is unacceptable and unprofessional. It comes from a place of assuming superiority, and that just couldn't fly with me.

The environment wasn't the best, having to become a minority all over again in the office. I know so many black professionals who quit their corporate jobs to work for themselves. With all the bias and covert racism that goes on, it just becomes quite tedious to deal with. I envied my white colleagues who would come into work to a floor full of people who looked like them, grew up like them and all shared similar interests. They would wake up every day and meet their genuine friends at work. Then they would go out drinking every other evening. It seemed like such fun for those who enjoyed it. I would have loved for work to be more fun for me. It could not have been more of a chore if it tried.

My friend Chris, who is part of the protest five, ended up leaving his job for these very reasons. He was hitting a glass ceiling and it had become quite tiresome trying to benefit from the same opportunities as other people but then having to stomach the bias that constantly pulled him back. Chris set up his own Brand Martial Arts locker room. He's been much happier since. The same can be said for me, even though it's meant less money. I'm happier now. Much happier. Towards the last few years of my time in the City, I was expiring. I believe that when you are young, and your sole focus is earning money; you care less about where you end up working. I know that at nineteen, with a new baby, I needed somewhere that paid well and that was that. However, as you get older, you desire something different for yourself. Something that'll fulfil your ambition. Perhaps this is the tugging of the heart that leads to what people call a mid-life crisis. That period in someone's life when they look at where they are and crave something different. Suddenly there are holes in your life and you go to the things that used to excite you to fill them up. We might want new sports cars or new partners. Luckily, I just wanted a new job. Perhaps I didn't actually. Perhaps what I wanted was to not be working in finance at all. But I knew that I still needed to work.

I was in my early forties when I changed my career. Three years before the transition, it became such a struggle to go to work. I just didn't want to do it anymore. I embraced the weekend as if I were a new divorcee. One and a half whole days of not being in the office. How tiny my bliss had become! Joy was locked in between Saturday morning and Sunday before 6 p.m. The moment Sunday morning dawned on me, so did the reality of work the following day. And the same again for the next five days. The thought would fill me with such trepidation and anxiety. Like evil clockwork, it would ruin my Sunday every week. On Monday mornings I'd wake up and fill my hands with a heavy head, then let it fall against my knees and mentally prepare for the day ahead. That was how I started almost every day. At 4.45 a.m., I'd be pulled from my dreams and forced into a concrete reality that flushed my body of all excitement. That is no way to live. The memory of those dark early mornings is enough to stop me from ever forcing my children into professions they hate. The average person spends one-third of their life at work, if not more. That's a large chunk of our lives here on earth to spend in resentment. Once I hit forty-two, I just couldn't do it anymore. I'm sure my performance levels dropped, too.

And yet, as much as I had grown irritated by everything about the office, truthfully, I didn't have the guts to leave. I had a mortgage and a few children to feed. Some would say it was luck, others would look at me today and say it was divine intervention … but my contract didn't get renewed at the Japanese bank I'd been at for four years. I was relieved. When I began to consider what to do next, a conversation I'd had with my brother really struck me. He worked in IT, too, but not in the City. He seemed far more at peace than I was, so I thought it might've been the City that was destroying me. The stress levels are much higher there and it reduces your work lifespan. You expire quickly – I can't repeat that enough. So I considered jobs outside of the City. I began a project manager job in Brentford. I had a six-month trial period and at the end we were in mutual agreement that the job wasn't for me. It was down to my performance at their end, but at mine I knew it just wasn't right for me. It turns out it wasn't to do with the City, it was IT.

We reflect the seasons in many ways – our skin becomes dry in winter just as the trees become barren of leaves, and as the air becomes hot so does our skin, just as summer hits its solstice. And just as the seasons pass, so do our stages of life. The sun had truly set on my IT career and it was time to give my future self a chance at realising its passion. After the amount of tension I'd lived with in the office, I didn't want to work for anybody else ever again. Personal training seemed like the perfect consolidation of all my new and old desires.

I've always cared about fitness, even when my mum said that it wouldn't pay. I've always cared about health and building strength and watching other people build strength. I just needed to get it down on paper to turn my hobby into a career. So I did a few certificates, one of which was a level-two gym-instructor qualification, followed by a level-three personal-training qualification. This included an anatomy and physiology exam. Yes, it was as tough as it sounds. I didn't know that I'd have to study the body to the same level as some junior doctors, so it did take a few attempts, but once I put my head down and studied properly, I passed.

I don't think I can really stress this enough, but when I was working in the City I was just surviving. And we have been convinced that this is the norm. To merely survive. To spend over half of our week so far removed from what

we were built to do. But to live without passion is to sleep with your eyes open. I believe that to live in service to your destiny is to live in service to your passion. We are all put here to do something. And now, as I approach fifty years old, it feels like my life is starting over again. Suddenly I'm posing for *Vogue* and *Men's Health*. People around me repeatedly say that I had to be at that protest because only I would have done what I did. I can't speak for anybody else, but it really was the only thing I *could* do. It was within me, just as your story sits within you, waiting for you to rub curious fingertips against the pages of your passion and eventually be brave enough to jump into the first chapter of your new wholesome life. Nobody can write the rest of your story except you. Now that I work in health, it feels as though I do so much more than survive. I wake up to half the money I was previously earning, but ten times the fulfilment. I have been blessed in abundance to be able to love my new career.

When I look at my younger two daughters today, I see a lot of myself in Sidéna in particular. I don't think she will stick with anything that she isn't in love with. She has the ability to become an actor, dancer or something in the arts. I can also see her in choreography or drawing. She's a born creative. I would be surprised if she got deep into academia, but she's still got some years to find out. As for Kendal, I'm not quite sure yet. If there is a role as a professional Roblox player, it is made for the lockdown edition of her! I reckon by Year 9 I'd like them to have a rough idea of what they might want to do as a first career. I'll try not to push them too hard down the route of academia. That goes for you, too, my grandchildren. I hope passion finds you early on and carries you into its future before anything of less interest gets a grip on you. The world is becoming so much bigger than a textbook and I trust that your intuition will lead you to know how to navigate it better than a fifty-year-old.

CHAPTER 6

HOME IS WHERE THE HEART IS ...

'As wholesome as I feel, I know that a large part of me remains a mystery. One that has the power to transform my entire identity.'

I cannot be sure of how old you will be when you begin reading this letter, my children and grandchildren. I use the latter title in a non-limiting sense. When I refer to grandchildren, I am also speaking to everyone and anyone who, like me, remains a student of life. A child to change. A canvas to be printed on. We are all grandchildren of the earth. I don't ever intend on sounding more philosophical than my lifestyle, but then perhaps life is nothing if not a game of chasing our philosophies, in the hope that when we finally live the life we've been dreaming of living, our ideas and our lifestyle will meet and fall into step, not disagree.

As humans we spend our hours, weeks and years chasing things. Pursuing the things we hope will increase our joy. Seeking new feelings that will replace old ones. Going to new places to fill the holes left by life's insistence on endings. I had a hole in my life growing up. Actually, it was more of an abyss. A vacuum, you could say. A vacuum in place of my father. The thing that differentiates a hole from a vacuum is the space's ability to pull everything into it or, on the other hand, wait for things to just fall in. Not having a father figure around forced things into me that perhaps would have circled the rim a few times and bounced away if he had been around. I did enjoy spending time with my mother's partner, Oliver, but he maintained an unoffensive distance out of respect for the fact that he was not my biological father.

Inevitably, questions were sucked into my DNA. Why isn't my own father around? How do I shave? What makes a man leave his son? How do I approach this girl that I like? What's the value of family? How do I change a tyre? In a dualistic world, questions are trailed by answers. They are not always the right answers, but how would I know? They were the only instructions to life that I had available. A blend of Mum's wisdom and my uncles' behaviour. This is what filled the vacuum that father created in his absence.

The thing about growing up without a dad is that it becomes apparent at various stages of your life. At thirteen you think you have grown accustomed to it, until you get into a fight with a boy on the estate and suddenly crave a father who can either help you fight or clean your wounds. In his absence, you may find yourself getting angry all over again. Boys channel that anger in different ways. Some channel it into women. Not always in an aggressive sense, but by searching – sometimes for love, sometimes for protection, sometimes to father her. Some boys channel it into numbness. Numbness towards relationships. Towards authority. Towards their mothers. Why couldn't Mum ensure that he stayed? For me? Resentment in its raw form is confusing. It's the emotional act of wishing something not to be the case, and hating that it is at the same time. I never resented my mum because my dad left. I loved her even more for deciding to love me with the charisma of both mother and father. I was one of the lucky ones, whose fatherless youth was just a shadow of the sun that lived in the heart of my mum. So while I didn't crave a dad as much as some boys might have, I really craved brothers. For years I wanted at least one older brother. Somebody who would stay. Somebody who would help me fight or clean the wounds. I guess in some ways that was another thing that was pulled into the vacuum. Funny story, though: I *did* have brothers. I just had no idea that home also existed a few roads down from my house until I was fifteen years old and sitting in a barber-shop chair.

A barber shop serves more than its main purpose of cutting hair. It does more than dish out skin fades, trims, cool partings and confidence. It's a place where men

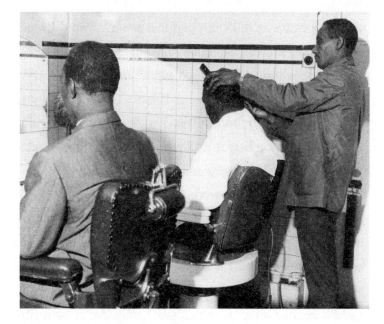

groom. Physically and often mentally. I think any space that is reserved for the betterment of one gender at a time can hold such a power. Men's meetings. Women's brunches. The nail salon. Football training.

Not only do we have our gender in common here, but we share a mutual desire to look and feel better than when we came in. That energy is unmatched.

It can be so freeing, to just be. I never wondered why some older men would just sit in the barber shop all day, dropping in and out of everybody else's conversations. It was fine to become part of the furniture. And it was also fine to become a spokesperson on just about anything. That's another thing I'd say about barber shops. If you put a microphone in the centre of the room, it would make for the most multifaceted podcast you ever heard. A place where everybody could be an expert, and nobody above the age of thirty-five was ever wrong. Nor were they all that teachable if I'm honest. You couldn't go to the barber's and not collect a fistful of laughs and outrageous opinions. There's no other place like it, really. Every two weeks my mum would take me to get my hair cut. Sometimes she would drop me off, tell the barber, Raymond, to look after me and then head out to run some errands. When I was much younger she would sometimes sit and wait. I think she stopped doing that as soon as she could. I'm not sure a barber shop was the best place for a beautiful woman. Too much testosterone. Testosterone that was too used to embracing its wildness within the walls of the shop.

As soon as I was allowed to go to places unaccompanied by an adult, I began to become an adult. I would walk myself to the barber shop, greet the other men myself, find my own seat, voice my own opinions when it felt appropriate. I would even sometimes have to remind the 'surgeons' that I was next in line when cheeky customers would try to take my spot in the chair. I call them 'surgeons' because the transformations that I witnessed in that chair were nothing short of an operation. They'd cut off the insecurity from the very tone of the black man's voice, lock admiration into our lungs, sharpen our self-confidence and then send us on our way. You could almost call it a form of therapy. You'd step out of the shop and hope to bump into at least one person. Chin slightly raised, chest slightly inflated, but a whole lot more grounded because you'd just left a room of men who looked like you. They lived like you. They ate the same oxtail, rice, peas and hard food. They had the same complaints about their mothers that I did. They had similar experiences with women. They didn't trust the government that much either. They weren't massive fans of the Chelsea Headhunters, who would pass through the estate every Saturday bringing an air of racism with them. They used the same patois-infused slang that I used. Some were my age. Some were me a few years before, back when my mum had to sit in with me. Some were me once I'd got a job after school. Some were young fathers. Some were me in twenty years. All of them were me before my hair started to desert me in my thirties. It was like a family tree without blood. I could track my years in that chair. The piece of wood on top of the chair that I had to sit on as a small boy got smaller and smaller as I got taller and taller. I understand why Inua Ellams made a theatre show called *Barber Shop Chronicles*. I understand why it sold out globally. I've always thought that the barber shop would make for fantastic reality TV. If not to entertain, then to show what black men are really like. If I was to pull myself apart and label the different parts of me with what they were influenced by, I'm sure there would be a section of my manhood with a barber-shop label on it. Not just because it was one of the only places where I was surrounded by fathers, but because, while sitting in the chair in the barber shop by my house that I had been going to every two weeks for as long as I'd had hair, I discovered that I had brothers. I had assumed that my siblings started and stopped with Pauline, but I was wrong.

I was fifteen years old. Of an age to take myself to the barber's. Finally. The barber shop was full. It looked like a pocket of carnival without the boomboxes and the sequins. I said my hellos to the regulars, spud a few of the younger boys and waited to get in the chair. As I waited, I caught my barber, Raymond, glancing over at me, as if he was trying to remember where he knew me from. I felt like saying, 'It's me, P ... from every other week for the past few years.' But that's not the kind of thing you say until an elder asks who you are. And he didn't, so I assumed maybe he was just stretching his neck. Although I knew he was taking in my face, and I'd soon find out why. As I climbed into the chair, he stood behind me and took in my face again in the mirror. He couldn't have been staring for more than a second before he said, 'Rahh, you are back already?' He was taking in the length of my hair with a confusion that I just couldn't place.

I said, 'What?'

Still picking at the length of my hair with the fingernail of an Afro comb, he remarked, 'You were here just a few days ago. Your hair grows back fast.'

Confused, I replied, 'No, I come every other week.' As far as I knew, it was quite usual to get a trim once a fortnight. I'd never considered my hair to grow particularly fast. I had white friends whose hair grew really long, but most black boys at the time would keep it low and 'neat' or have it in cornrows. Mum wasn't too keen on long hair. But Raymond was adamant. He was turning to his colleagues to confirm that I had in fact been sitting in that same chair just two days before.

In true barber-shop fashion, everybody with a pulse became involved in the conversation. 'Yeah, yeah, yeah, I seen him just two days ago.' It seemed like everybody had seen me here except me. I even second guessed myself for a moment.

Perhaps I'd popped in and forgotten about it. But then, no! I definitely hadn't had my hair cut for around two weeks. I could tell by my raggedy hairline. 'Nah, Raymond, it wasn't me.'

He took in my face in the mirror one last time and then asked, 'Do you have a brother?'

You know when you put your hand in your pocket to find something and you're rummaging around until you prick your finger on something sharp? That's what it felt like when he asked if I had a brother. I wish. 'No, I don't.' He asked if I was sure, and it was at that exact moment that I realised I was only as sure as I could be, having never really known my father.

A hush fell over the entire world as he asked his next question, which ended up changing my life. A question that felt as foreign as French. 'What's your dad's name?' I reluctantly responded with a name that felt equally as foreign on my tongue. My dad's name didn't feel very nice passing through my lips.

'WAH DI BUMBACLART!' the world screamed. Carnival had erupted again within these walls. Every barber with a head to attend to had stopped what they were doing to express wild shock in their own unique way. It was like an electric current had stopped at the door of the shop and decided it would become a firework. That's what my stomach felt like. Fireworks. Or perhaps grenades. Something less colourful.

'YOU HAVE A BROTHER, DONOVAN, HE LIVES AROUND HERE!' Raymond bellowed, as if he had just cracked the Da Vinci Code. While the room vibrated in excitement at this *Jeremy Kyle* moment, Raymond found my brother's number and insisted I call him. I'm sure the shop would have loved me to call him right there and then with my phone on loud speaker. This was exactly the kind of drama that could only be executed in a barber shop. Or on reality TV. Which is exactly what it felt like at that moment. Raymond could have cut a Nike tick across my forehead and I might not have realised. As I sat in the chair clutching the scrap of lined paper that was becoming a towel for my sweaty palms, I couldn't think straight. I couldn't even finish a thought. *How? Who? When? Does Mum know? How do I tell Pauline?* I had so many questions. Questions whose answers were trapped between my palm and eleven digits. I wished I could have teleported to my house once my hair was cut. My legs were too small for my liking. My strides too short for how quickly I wanted to reach my house. My home. The place where I lived with my family. My mum and my sister Pauline. The only family I'd ever known.

Opening my front door felt strange. Not because I was worried, but because I knew something very significant had just happened, and there was a thin chance that the next time I walked out of my house, it would be into a new life. One that included a boy called Donovan, with whom I shared facial features.

I wasted no time in asking my mother what the barber was talking about. I can't remember exactly how I was feeling at this point. Whether I wanted Mum to just say that the barber says all kinds of crazy things and I didn't have a brother who lived a few roads away. Or whether I wanted Mum to feel exactly how I was feeling. She responded with neither. Sure, a part of her was a bit shocked, but it's not like she gasped. It was more like an exhale. I suppose she knew that my dad had probably had other children. For two months I didn't say anything to anyone about this. I didn't call the number and I didn't tell my friends. I was far too scared to suddenly face the possibility that I shared the same blood with other boys. I wish I had kept a journal of those two months, just to be able to look back at how I felt towards this unknown brother, who I've since come to love dearly.

One day in the park, I ended up in a fight with another child. To anybody watching, I was winning. But as is the nature of a fight, one minute I was triumphing over him, the next minute I was getting beaten up. It all happened so fast, I didn't notice that the other child had his older brothers there. Whenever I was on top of the boy, they would pull me off and put their brother on top. That day, as I carried my bruised limbs home with me, I really wished I had a brother. So once I got home, I stopped any intrusive thoughts and just bit the bullet. I called my brother. And he picked up. My brother picked up. Donovan picked up. He had a deep voice. Deeper than mine, at least, and he could not believe the story I was telling him about the barber shop. Again, I wish I had recorded the call or something, because we'd both love to listen to it back.

We arranged to meet up that evening. He came with his dog Prince and another brother, Peter, who had a Jamaican accent that you could recognise anywhere. They came back to our maisonette and met my mother and sister – their sister. I genuinely believe that the energy we tapped into that evening could have organised an entire family reunion that same day. I wish we had. Instead, we laughed, gasped and greeted each other with the love that can only come from sharing blood. I was itching to meet my other brother, so we left my mum's and headed towards their house to meet my older brother, Roy.

They resembled me. We looked alike. I looked like my brothers. And what was funny was that I realised I'd seen Donovan before. Plenty of times, actually. I had walked past him so many times on the way to school. I'd seen him on the 77a bus, which ran from Wandsworth Road (where I lived) to Clapham Junction. He would get on the bus at Lavender Hill with a Burberry scarf wrapped around his mouth. I remember this distinctly because I had also decided that I didn't like him very much. He had what we called a 'screwface'. His default face was that of a frown. I never liked the way he looked at me, so I'd decided I also didn't like him. I was fifteen and that was

My brothers, Donovan and Roy.

how things were back then. As if that wasn't already ironic enough, as time passed and more and more people started to hear that we were brothers, more and more dots were connected. We shared so many mutual friends who also never suspected that we were brothers. Today, I wonder how they couldn't. We looked so, so similar. The Evans brothers – Philip, Anthony, Edward and Jason – should have pondered on the resemblance at least once. Anthony and Edward were tremendous body poppers and would always try to teach me, but I was never as good as them.

141

Edward also helped ignite my love affair with hip-hop music and created tons of mixed tapes for me. Edward was like a gentle giant and I really looked up to him. Funnily enough, almost as you would an older brother. It turns out I was only slightly off the mark. He was my brother's best friend! There was also Geoffrey and Eddie Gayle, who also knew both my brother and me. And then there was Matthew, who literally lived next door to me and was best mates with Roy! So my brother Roy would literally have been hanging outside my front door without knowing of the family tree that lived just a few metres away.

Perhaps even more Hollywood … my mum used to keep a photo of her and my father in a photo album. I think it was one of the only photographs that I'd seen of them together. Naturally, my father's face was stained across my eyes. It was the only time I saw him. I had remembered seeing Donovan on my walks to school and thinking that he looked just like my dad did in that photograph. Turns out he did. They shared more than the same features. In fact, we all did.

Beyond blood, we got on like a house on fire. We had so much in common. My brothers and I, that is. I don't know about my dad. I'm not sure how it went down with him, this meeting, but I know that my new eldest brother was angry about not being told he had siblings living so close. I heard from Donovan that he absolutely lost it with my father that evening. Understandably. Given how close we all lived, what if we had got into fights with each other? Or worse. What if Pauline had dated one of them? For a period, my mind ran wild with rage. I do wish I could have joined Roy in laying into our dad, but if I'm honest, I was just so happy to have siblings. I had always wanted a brother. Suddenly, at the drop of a hat, I had three. How many people get to say that? It was like the Christmas family party that never ended. You might be reading this letter wondering how on earth I sat on my brother's number for months before calling, but today I'm confident that there was an appointed time for me to call. The fight with the white child was just a catalyst; that was always going to be when I gave in to that curiosity. I had got to that age when my sister Pauline was really annoying me. I'd be out sometimes and see her wearing my clothes. It just seemed like we were suddenly always in each other's way. Finding out that we had other siblings was the best thing that could have happened at that time. Suddenly we had other places to direct our energy.

Donovan and Roy introduced us to our new sisters: Susan, Paula, Pamela, Julia and Samantha. Altogether with Pauline and Peter, there are 10 of us, and if you saw us today, you'd never assume that we missed the first fifteen years of each other's lives. They are like my best friends. The siblings I'd always wanted, and eventually found. Lives like ours inspire the fairy tales. This was the definition of a happy ending. I was so nervous meeting them at first, but the oddest thing broke the ice between me and Donovan. In true teenage-boy fashion, our trainers became the main focus of our first meeting. Trainers were a really big thing in the mid-eighties. I'm sure they still are among the younger generation. I was so proud of my ZX 7-10s. I was even more proud of them when I saw that Donovan only had the ZX 5-50s. I did love that we shared the same shoes, though. It was almost symbolic of us having walked the same roads, having the same family tree and the same story. He loved it, too. Or at least he was impressed. Perhaps he was slightly jealous, I don't know. I never got the vibe that he was the kind of brother to compete with me. Well, I did at one point actually. But it made me who I am today, so we laugh about it now.

Donovan is one of the first reasons I ever got into fitness as a teenager. Having siblings was amazing. I could go to their houses and feel like I had another home. One day I went up to Donovan's room and he was getting changed. Before he could pull his T-shirt over his head, I caught a glimpse of his chest. It just looked so defined and pumped. It caught my gaze in a way that a woman's chest might have at that age. I was so taken aback that I asked him about it. I asked if he was gyming or doing push-ups. He dismissed it and said that he wasn't and then pulled his shirt over his evidently worked-out chest. I didn't think much of it, but I did take in my own chest in the mirror that evening. A few days later I went over again and his grandad, Da-Da, opened the door. I took my usual route upstairs, but there was nothing usual about his room when I got there. Donovan had a whole bench out underneath him, a set of weights in both hands and the expression of a man who had just been caught red-handed. Or heavy-handed in this case. I couldn't believe it. The man was hiding the plug. He had been getting buff behind closed doors and, for whatever reason, he wasn't telling me about it.

Despite the attention he was getting for his mysterious gains, I'm sure Donovan was happy that I found out, because it meant that he now had a training partner. We started lifting weights together at his house during the week, growing, bonding and building. The weights belonged to our big brother Roy, but he didn't seem to want to use them. Which was great for us, until it wasn't. We ended up becoming so hooked on the growth that we outgrew them. The weights stopped being heavy enough and we needed to up our dosage if we wanted to maintain and build further. This is when I would say my life started. Or at least a very large chapter of it. We joined our first gym together. It was Brixton Recreation Centre in South

London. This is actually where I first met Jamaine, one of the protest five. Jamaine would let the youngsters who couldn't afford to train in through the back door. I guess you could say that Jamaine was my first introduction to activism through sport and Donovan was my first introduction to brotherhood in sport. Two lessons that have gone on to shape and save my life. I suppose that is what family is supposed to do. Advance your life.

Donovan and I became inseparable for around ten years until after we both became fathers. Home stretched itself beyond all that we'd known and suddenly began to spread across London. Now that we all have children and some of our children are having children, home continues to spread its wings across London – 60 per cent of my family live there. Around 30 per cent live in Jamaica and the rest in the US. London has always felt like home to me. I know that, as a concept, to belong somewhere is so personal and intricate. But to me, home is where the heart knows, and my heart beats for my family. They encourage my very pulse. They fill my cheeks with laughter and my days with smiles. How can home be anywhere else? When I hear racist people suggesting that us black folk should go back home, I'm always confused. My mother lives here and so does her mum. Home isn't the starting point of skin. Home is where skin gets to hang itself up for the day and melt into a sofa. To pull back socks with a big toe and be surrounded by love. London has been that place for me for fifty years. I know that it comes with its bias, but it's still mine. Even if it doesn't want to be.

When I visit Jamaica, I'm reminded of how much of a Londoner I am. From how the patois always struggles to fit between my lips to just about stomaching the spices used in the food.

While these stamps of being British can be concealed, some things are obvious, and my Jamaican family never let me forget it. They call us 'English boys' when we come over. It's funny, because an English person would never claim me. They would call me Jamaican. They would ask where I was *really* from, after I tell them I'm from South London. The diaspora exists on the equator line. We aren't fully accepted anywhere. This is made apparent everywhere we go. That being said, I see this as a luxury. I am rich in culture. Rich in the Premier League and rich in cricket. Rich in fish and chips and rich in saltfish fritters. I basically get to exist twice. English people only get to be English and Jamaicans in Jamaica only get to be Jamaican. I get to pull from both cultures whenever I want, and that is a blessing as far as I'm concerned. Don't they say that two is always better than one? I can think of only a few examples where that isn't the case. Although the question of retirement does pop up. When you're young you can bounce from place to place, but as you become old and frail, you have to really consider this idea of 'home' again. I'm not sure if I'd want to retire in London. I don't even think Londoners want to retire in London. I'd rather spend my last years somewhere with sunshine, fresh fruit and food that won't kill me quicker than necessary. I've got a desire to explore more Caribbean islands.

Who knows, maybe I'll spend the last quarter of my life in St Vincent. There is so much of the world I'm yet to explore, I can't think of where I'd want to retire just yet. I know that I still have years of travelling Africa to do. If we were to refer to home in an ancestral way, Africa is home. That is where my roots are. That's where all of our roots are.

It has always confused me when Africans and Caribbeans argue. Especially when the argument begins with Caribbeans saying that they aren't African. If you trace our history back, a lot of us were taken from Africa. But our history on the islands precedes slavery. We existed as Native Americans before the pirate Christopher Columbus 'discovered' the islands in the hope of finding gold. The Englishmen who had captured much of Jamaica continued to ship Africans over to Jamaica to man the fields and further the sugar and tobacco industry. There was something about the build and strength displayed that enticed Englishmen to exploit these people. Amid all the movement, those who were enslaved rebelled many times. In an attempt to reclaim ownership, the English and Spanish carried out a long process of stripping Jamaicans of their cultural practices, religions and, most heartbreakingly of all, their names. You take a man's name, you uproot the trail of his history. Once names were changed to match the slave owners, many slaves were shipped across to England to start new lives as Edwins, Georges and Charlestons. This is why so many Caribbeans have such English last names. We adopted a lineage that was forced upon us, and we gave it to our children. My deepest regret is not discovering my African name before having my own children. I would have loved to start a family tree that did not carry the seed of our oppressors. My forefathers are not Hutchinsons. Although I do not know what they were called. While Malcom X was in prison, he rejected his slave name and took up the name 'X'. In doing so, he famously reminded those of the revolution that, 'A race of people is like an individual man; until it uses its own talent, takes pride in its own history, expresses its own culture, affirms its own self-hood, it can never fulfil itself.'

As wholesome as I feel, I know that a large part of me remains a mystery. One that has the power to transform my entire identity. Growing up, I would cringe when it came to writing my name on things. It was a constant reminder that I was wearing my slave master's investment around my identity like a bow. So much of my history was erased along with my name. Hutchinson does not tell the story of my true, rich lineage. I can guess where in Africa I would have come from, but ultimately I carry the name of my oppressors. And this troubles me deeply.

From the melanin that wraps itself around my bones like a poster, I know that I am African, but I do not know where in Africa I am from. Sometimes I see my name as a question mark. Sometimes it asks me, 'How did we let our history be burnt away like this?' Other times it begs to be crossed out and replaced with something that can bring with it a sweeter story than slavery. Through carrying on the slave name, my identity is labelled as inferior. Sometimes it wakes the mental contentions over what Africa must have been, in comparison to how it is recorded today. It is not all flies and villages. Africa is not AIDS and Western intervention. I know that I descend from a continent of plenty. Plenty of land and plenty of resources. Our world map has been manipulated to show Africa to be fourteen times smaller than it actually is. This is all part of cementing the superiority complexes that cloud the English. But I see beyond it.

I've never felt the urgency to survive or compete with others. This must be something deep in the black psyche, inherited from our ancestors. I might not be able to put my finger on it, but I know in my gut that we were the epitome of regality and the envy of the world. This is why I struggle to understand the moral compass of men from other lands who perceive me to be inferior and seek to do me harm. I am seen as a threat and so others feel the need to control and defeat me. I guess the moral superiority that some folk will never admit to is as much a blessing as it is a curse, as not everyone plays by the same rules. I've been dehumanised and treated as though I do not contribute to civilisation. Yet so much of civilisation was birthed in the palm of Africa. Genetically, it's my understanding that traces of me, my children and you, my grandchildren, can be found all over the world. In 2020, a relearning is taking place. So many young Africans from the diaspora are travelling home for the 'years of return'. Concepts of Africa are being revised and reclaimed by the true gatekeepers of the land. I suppose that is the beauty of time's consistency. In its eternal nature, there is always an opportunity for what was once lost to be reclaimed.

I feel a glimmer of this with my name. Since seeing it in magazines and news reports, attached to the Black Lives Matter movement, it's as if a new weight has been added to it. Patrick Hutchinson. The man who exposes the deeply empathetic nature of black people. I have started to like it again over the past few months, and I cannot tell you how much of a relief that is for me. To sign my signature and know that it now stands for something beyond a slave master.

Today it epitomises blackness. And that is a 360 that I can quietly take pride in.

CHAPTER 7

THE OUTCRY

'If racism can be taught, it can then be unlearnt.'

Of all the surprises that the year 2020 brought with it, the new face of allyship was by far the most shocking to me. Friends and old colleagues of different ethnicities that had peacefully avoided the race conversation were suddenly protesting, calling out micro-aggressions against people that looked like me and joining arms with those oppressed because of their race.

Everything about it pulled my eyes open a bit wider. Why was everyone so inspired to suddenly change the racist world? By 2020, there had been a racially charged murder video being shared every other day. If it wasn't a black mother being stopped, manhandled and tasered by police in front of her children, it was a young black boy being shot multiple times at close range for 'looking suspicious'. There had never been a lack of reason to protest unfortunately.

This time, however, it seemed as though people were finally being re-sensitised to the displays of discrimination and were waking up to their own complicity. I can hazard a guess as to what provoked the sudden urge to speak out that seemed to explode from lips that had never uttered a word about race before. For one, perhaps it was the first time some people had actually had the willingness to watch a police brutality video. On any busy day of our very busy lives, we can just about carry our own issues through those twenty-four hours, let alone those of others. It's easier to mentally block the images, videos and statistics that flood the Internet, which constantly remind us that the world is a very unfair place to exist. Between eight-hour work days, raising children and trying to cultivate a social life, it's not uncommon for people to filter what they consume and what will leave an impression on their moral compass. But in 2020, during the few months that surrounded the vicious murder of George Floyd, there was no distraction big or important enough to come before such a heinous display of injustice.

Some people had been furloughed from work. Others were told to work from home. But one thing reigned true. Everybody was spending more time on their phones. With the global population going into a strict lockdown, our social-media feeds became our window onto the world. We had no restaurants, so everybody became an

Instagram chef. The wind carried the scent of more banana bread than ever before. The gyms were closed and nobody was travelling to work. We met our real eating habits face to face. We sweated in our living rooms and posted the body progress on our feeds. We compared our body type to the fitness YouTubers and allowed ourselves to feel pressured into transition. Triggered. That is what we all suddenly had time to become. This was the major difference in the spread of activism. People suddenly had fewer distractions and more space to finally come to terms with a very broken world. Perhaps it was the very fact that everybody's lives had been somewhat displaced that created an air of unity. In some ways, we were all in this together. Not a race war, but a war of some kind. Whether it was a war against coronavirus, or a war against our government's handlings of it all. For once, we were all experiencing the same thing. We were all stuck at home. We were all worried. We were all confused. We were all online. We all saw the video of a black man being suffocated under the knee of a policeman in broad daylight. And in our new sense of shared humanity, we were all outraged.

I cried when I first saw the video. George Floyd was treated worse than an animal while passers-by recorded and watched. Can we take a moment to really understand that, away from the necessary hysteria of our reaction? A human. A dad. A son's neck. Hold your own. Put your palm to the side of your neck and apply a bit of pressure. Imagine your hand was a knee. Hold your own. Apply a bit of pressure. That knee was pressing the weight of a full-grown man into the delicate neck of an innocent man who was left to cry out for his mother. The policeman kept his hands in his pocket as if squeezing the life from another human was as casual as waiting for a balloon to deflate. George Floyd cried out, 'I can't breathe.' Every single person there could see that he was unarmed and not a threat, yet the policeman continued to press the life out of George Floyd's throat. What possesses a man to think that he can so gruesomely kill another man, in broad daylight, with his hands in his pockets, looking directly into the camera? It is impossible not to be outraged. Not to be furious. Not to be hurt. Not to put yourself in the shoes of his mother. His daughter. His friends. Who now have to watch the video of their loved one being killed over and over again. I can only imagine the trauma. There is no peace there. There is no dignity in his death for his family to ever find closure.

Whether this was the first video of its kind or a weekly subscription for people, what was mutual was the heartbreak. For some, it led to a repost of the video with an emotional, humanist caption. '*Why can't we all just get along?*' For others, it was frustration with the frequency

of such tragedies. What I found to be very different this time was that the latter group suddenly had eager listeners. People had removed the wool from their ears and started to listen to the experiences and voices of those who speak about race. For so many, this was a first. On both sides of the conversation.

White people were messaging their black friends with everything from apologies to messages of solidarity to questions on how to become an ally. Asian people were pulling up their parents on their historically discriminative syntax and stereotypes. MPs were collecting signatures to reopen racist inquiries. CEOs of banks were sending emails around to their employees encouraging free speech and offering resources on how to actively 'not be racist'. I'd honestly never seen anything like it. It was like a live wire had just landed in the ocean and illuminated racism for the first time. It truly did feel like, even if just for a few weeks, everyone was against racism. It seemed like we had finally reached a place where real change could occur. The entire world protested. There were more people on the streets than ever before in history. I was so gobsmacked to see the number of white, Chinese, Asian and Hispanic communities that had come out to protest that day and every other day. There were information packs going viral on where to donate, how to support black communities, which books to read and what films to watch to inform the cause. White people were looking in the mirror and, for the first time, seeing the privilege that had always cloaked their skeleton in the form of skin. There was a shared sense of guilt that I could tangibly feel from many white communities.

They were reading the statistics on employee discrimination. Watching the police brutality videos. Thinking of the lovely black people they knew and feeling bad because they looked like the oppressor. It did expose some weird corners of whiteness, however. I saw a very odd video of around forty white people in America, kneeling down in front of the black members of their community and 'denouncing their privilege'. White TikTok stars filmed themselves crying on camera over the injustices caused by people that looked like them. The US Democrats all draped a West African printed stole around their necks before taking a knee for eight minutes, ahead of the passing of a bill that would ban the use of chokeholds by law enforcers. There was no shortage of odd gestures being made. But I do know that the silver lining of misguided guilt is its willingness to be directed. People were listening. They were asking questions and demanding justice for those who didn't share the same skin colour. And for so many black people, it was the shift we knew was necessary if we ever wanted real change to occur. We'd been shouting for equality our whole lives, but sometimes it did feel like we were the only ones hearing each other. Bitter thanks to a global pandemic and a heartbreaking tragedy, the world woke up.

I saw a quote that seemed to act as a foundation for much of the new activism that had begun. It was originally said by Desmond Tutu. 'If you are neutral in situations of injustice, you have chosen the side of the oppressor.' Nobody with sense wanted to be on the side of the oppressor, so people spoke out. Some for the first time, some for the fiftieth.

According to Google, allyship has been defined as 'a lifelong process of building relationships based on trust, consistency, and accountability with marginalized individuals and/or groups of people'. One person who fits this description in a groundbreaking way is Jane Elliott. A former school teacher and lifelong educator.

The year 1968 was a landmark year for several reasons. *Apollo 8* orbited the moon for the first time. Students across the globe protested against the Vietnam War. Robert F. Kennedy was assassinated. And perhaps most notably, Dr Martin Luther King Jr was shot on his balcony by a troubled James Earl Ray. The days following the killing of the famous 'I have a dream' civil-rights activist were rife with riots and rage. Especially when there was speculation that, after he was rushed into hospital with bullet wounds, Dr King was then suffocated by a pillow or killed within the very walls that were meant to save his life. The streets screamed for justice to be served. The police began what became one of the biggest manhunts in history, stretching over two months and five countries to eventually find the shooter in London. Also in the year 1968, in a small town in Iowa, parents gathered at their children's school to witness one brave teacher's attempt to challenge the discrimination that had become so prominent in the US.

Shortly after the killing of Dr Martin Luther King Jr, Jane Elliott attempted to replicate the judgement that leads to such racial division in a classroom of white, prejudiced children. She segregated the class on the premise of eye colour. On the first day of the experiment, she convinced the class that those with blue eyes were superior to those with brown eyes. Jane Elliott persuaded the class that those with brown eyes were dumb and unworthy. She prohibited the children with brown eyes from drinking from the fountain and gave them a shorter lunch break, as well as smaller lunch servings. On the flipside, she empowered the children with blue eyes. She told them that they were more intelligent, more deserving and far more superior. She then made the brown-eyed children wear a collar around their necks to signal their inferiority.

Over the course of the day, the children began to display unusual resentments towards each other. Judgements on their classmates that had never existed before were placed in a hierarchy. There were tears, fights in the playground and bruised egos. One girl ran out crying because she was so upset about being discriminated against. As a black person in a white world, the only place you can run is back into the racist world. In fifteen minutes, the parents – and millions of watchers years later – witnessed a class of thoughtful, well-behaved children become monsters. On day two, Jane convinced the class that she had got it wrong, and in fact it was those with brown eyes who were superior. We watched an immediate switch of attitude take place, as the children with brown eyes became happier, ruder and more confident. Jane Elliott used cards to assess how these complexes can manifest in several ways. On the day that the brown-eyed children were taught to be inferior, they took five minutes to work through a pack of cards that Jane Elliot had based a task on, while those with blue eyes took two minutes. On day three, when the roles were reversed, the brown-eyed children only took two minutes to work through the cards, while the blue-eyed children's time lengthened to four minutes and eighteen seconds. When asked why they took longer on the second day, the children remarked that they were 'dumb' or 'focused on their collars'. Jane's experiment had exposed how easily prejudice can be taught and learnt, in an effort to display how easily it can be unlearnt at a young age. She said that 'racism is ignorance based on being miseducated. Racism is a result of being indoctrinated instead of educated.' Since then, Jane Elliott has continued to rebuke colour-blindness and inform racists of their miseducation and often unconscious bias.

More and more Jane Elliotts were created in the year 2020. Big brands suddenly came under pressure from consumers to show solidarity. Especially brands that seemed to benefit from black culture. Some companies were forced to expose the racial breakdown of their boardrooms. Embarrassingly, some had to issue statements that went along the lines of 'we won't share our employee information, because we know how much we need to improve'. The people had regained their power, and in fear of being boycotted and blacklisted, brands had to make their position on inequality very clear or vow to do better as an establishment. Some companies turned out to have been friends of the movement the entire time. It came to the surface that the well-known ice-cream brand Ben & Jerry's were not new to activism. Years before, in 2016, after the fatal shooting of Keith Lamont Scott, Ben & Jerry's publicly encouraged their customers to become well versed in the racism of the country. In 2019 and 2020, on 20 April, a day known as 4/20, when marijuana is celebrated every year across the world, Ben & Jerry's used the opportunity to reveal the racial injustices within the cannabis industry. That might be a bit weird to read, but I'll explain it later in this letter. Their activism did not stop at the plain-black screen that plastered social media on 2 June 2020. They filled the screen with the words 'We must dismantle white supremacy'. They included a four-step guide that suggested 'calling on President Trump to commit the US to a formal process of healing and reconciliation, asking Congress to create a commission to study the effects of slavery and discrimination from 1619 to the present and supporting the Floyd family's call to create a national task force that would draft bipartisan legislation aimed at ending racial violence and increasing police accountability'. While some people were upset that they didn't post the plain-black screen, in the words of the London poet Sophia Thakur, 'I understand the power of unity, but imagine if we were all united in action and not silent black screens.' Action became the defining method of identifying who was really about the cause and who just didn't want to get bad press. Brands such as Nike, who have historically donated to and endorsed those who have been discriminated against, rose to the occasion. The power of such big brands standing up and taking action is one that trickles down to their consumers. The average person may be confused or perhaps too shy to speak out against the system, but seeing celebrities and global companies take such unapologetic action can liberate that fear and inspire the activist within. The same can be said, unfortunately, for those who oppose any great and progressive movement. As those on the right side of history became more empowered, so did those whose hatred is fuelled by the very idea of equality.

The essence of balance is that where there is light, there is darkness. Where there are tears over oppression, there are cheers from the oppressors. This became unnervingly evident in the months following the protest. Since everyone was online and expecting some kind of opinion or statement from just about everybody with a platform, some views were revealed to be part of the problem. It was as if some people could see a black man be murdered in broad daylight and still be convinced that black people were the problem. At so many points during these protests I felt helpless, because if the statistics alone did not bring to light the need for transformation, then a graphic video really should have been able to shatter any denial and break out the humanity in people. Where this failed, I did lose a lot of faith for a period. What more did somebody need to see to understand that this was wrong? How many more black bodies needed to line the streets before some people became convinced that there was a huge problem plaguing our society? How much more blood? How many more mothers' tears?' I survive by believing that if racism can be taught, it can then be unlearnt. But what else can be said to make those opposed to equality take a step back and revise their bias? What will make a person understand that the mindset they so desperately aim to defend is the very mindset that is killing innocent people and breaking lives apart? It's more than just a racist tweet. It's more than an inappropriate comment and reinforced stereotype. These very things validate the behaviour of racists. On the Internet, some people call it 'trolling', but I think we've lost sight of how powerful the Internet can be in justifying and validating dangerous rhetoric.

If you are of the belief that the media has its own autonomous agenda, I can understand why. As my boys and I sat at Eat of Eden that evening following the protest, we were all wondering how the media would cover the day. Would the newspapers do their usual job of finding the pin-drop of black-on-black violence that occurred at a largely peaceful protest? They did. Would they show videos of the hundreds of white men chanting racist chants and throwing all kinds of objects at the police? They did not. For many, seeing me on the front cover was a huge relief. It was a headline that would not take away from the movement, but instead paint black people in a more positive light. I wonder whether the video and photo would have made all those headlines and covers if I'd been carrying a black boy. Perhaps not. The media seems to reject any opportunity to promote the positive things that happen when a black person is involved. And in the cases where they do talk about something that is inherently good, there seems to always be a negative twist on the matter.

Raheem Sterling, the Manchester City and England football player, spoke out against this last year. He is an exceptional talent with a beautiful family, but the British media have used every opportunity to create an ugly picture of him as a man. In fact, Sterling took to Instagram to compare the press coverage of two players doing the exact same thing: buying their mother a house. Same newspaper, same sport, same act of kindness, but completely different headlines. The *Daily Mail* headline that covered the story of the young black player read: 'Young Manchester City footballer, 20, on £25,000 a week, splashes out on mansion on market for £2.25 million despite having never started a Premier League match.' The headline that covered the white player read: 'Manchester City starlet Phil Foden buys new £2 million home for his mum', with the tagline 'Manchester City's Phil Foden has set up his future in the area by buying a new house'. This is only one example of thousands of displays of micro-racism that occurred last year. Raheem Sterling has been scrutinised for having a wife and family at a young age. He has been torn apart by the press for buying himself nice things while simultaneously being ridiculed for shopping at Primark. And that's just off the pitch. On the pitch, he has been verbally abused by other players and fans for the colour of his skin. Although he usually ignores the behaviour of the press, he took to Instagram to explain why this was a slippery slope for the country. 'This young black child is looked at in a bad light. Which helps fuel racism and aggressive behaviour, so for all the newspapers that don't understand why people are racist in this day and age all I have to say is have a second thought about fair publicity and give all players an equal chance.'

Racism within the space of certain British sports has become so normalised that many people's response was, 'It's football culture.' But throwing a banana at a player on the pitch while calling him a monkey is not the kind of culture that should be allowed to continue. In a BBC Radio 5 Live interview, Darren Lewis stated, 'It's what we've become used to over the years because football hasn't done enough to protect black players on the field of play, and fans have become increasingly emboldened to go to football matches and vent. We've created what we loosely term as "atmosphere", but within that whole culture anything goes and people do invariably cross the line. People feel that they can go to live television games where they know they will be in full view and malign the footballers in the way that they do.' He writes for the *Daily Mirror* and has also issued statements accusing them of brushing the complaints they receive about race under the rug. The truth of the matter is this: black rage is highly profitable. Not just black rage, but anything discriminatory that puts black people at the detriment of the product and in a corner of reaction and retaliation. As a writer, you can trust that if you openly demonise a section of society, there will be a community of people who were simply waiting for an opportunity to have their own problematic views emboldened and validated. In Britain, when the Brexit campaign first kicked off and we had politicians promising to send migrants back to their place of origin, we saw a huge spike in racial hate crime. I'm led to believe that media personalities such as Katie Hopkins are strategically protected, despite the sheer levels of abuse they hurl at almost every section of society.

After all, Katie Hopkins has spewed racial, fatphobic and every other kind of phobic rhetoric across all social-media channels, yet somehow she has not met with even a quarter of the disciplinary action that artists such as Wiley have received for targeting the Jewish community. Within a week of tweeting about the Jewish community, he had all of his social-media channels deleted, and his earnings from them removed, and he was not granted any further interviews, as Katie Hopkins so often is. Most surprisingly, he was banned from the new social-media app TikTok. Despite millions of complaints and boycotts, TikTok has refused to implement a rule that stops content creators from making offensive videos. TikTok has normalised the use of 'black face', domestic violence, racist language and so many other weeds of the world. What scares me the most is that it is an app used predominantly by children.

They are being exposed to 'funny' videos that show white children hanging their black friends from a tree or chaining them up and whipping them. I look at my younger daughters and wonder what could ever bring them to a point of behaving in such a hurtful way, and I struggle to imagine how those children online have been raised and what they have been taught about humanity. I guess this is just another way in which privilege manifests itself. My younger daughters wouldn't dream of treating somebody with less respect just because of their skin colour. I guess they have never been in a position to even exercise such superiority. As it should be across all races. And ages, for that matter. The problem with giving racists any kind of platform is that it validates that backwards way of thinking. Some people just don't like black people, and they can't really explain why. And then they come across a Tommy Robinson video or statement, find the justification they're looking they're looking for and lean further into that flawed way of thinking. Whenever I think about some of the things that man has been allowed to say, it really does astonish me. I think, as black people, we'd rather be shocked than upset. There's a quote I read once that really sums up how I feel. It said: 'To be a Negro in this country and to be relatively conscious is to be in a state of rage almost, almost all of the time.' And it's true. Right now, from where I'm sitting, there are African migrants being dropped in the middle of the ocean. There are news channels getting close enough to put a microphone in their wet faces, but they are not offering aid. A mother was shot repeatedly in her home as she slept by police who are yet to be charged. There is a huge child-trafficking scandal being carried out on some of the biggest online-shopping websites. Vaccines for viruses are being tested on poor villagers in Africa, causing children to die and women to become infertile. There is a live and active slave trade happening in Lebanon and across the Middle East. The world is full of race-fuelled tragedy that, if meditated on, will break any beating heart into pieces.

That's why I try to stay away from constantly consuming black trauma. It cannot be healthy to remain in a place of such rage. I'm not sure I'm built for it. I'm triggered too easily, perhaps. I remember the month of October last year did everything it could to unsettle me during what was supposed to be a month celebrating blackness. Gucci released a $890 polo-neck sweatshirt that looked just like a golliwog. Any level of racial sensitivity would have told at least one of the many people working at Gucci that this was a problematic design. A golliwog was a doll created from the 'Negro minstrel' doll. These dolls were used to depict black children and people as ugly. Almost animalistic. Sometimes the dolls were made with paws instead of hands. The stories surrounding these dolls would depict them as mean-spirited and very unkind.

They became very popular across Britain and Europe during some of the most racist periods of history. The crude attempt at displaying African features as beastly has caused these dolls to be banned in so many countries, yet somehow one of the largest high-fashion brands in the world still chose to release the new design – during Black History Month. That, to me, seems intentional.

What makes a person want to bask in other people's hurt? Why does that excite some people? Perhaps it's the thrill of getting away with it. Or perhaps it's evidence of a one-colour boardroom that didn't have any diverse thoughts or experiences that would tell them that this was problematic.

Apparently this was the case for the recent H&M debacle. The high-street clothing brand was releasing a new collection of children's clothes. They photographed a young black boy wearing a shirt that said '*Coolest monkey in the jungle*'. Now, I understand that children are always called cheeky monkeys, but the term when associated with black people has always been used in a derogatory and offensive way. Footballers are often taunted with monkey noises or have physical bananas thrown at them. After the shirt caused a social-media uproar, H&M appointed their first diversity officer to oversee the campaigns and hiring structures in the Swedish-run company. They also released a statement saying, 'We have got this wrong and we agree that, even if unintentional, passive or casual racism needs to be eradicated wherever it exists.' It exists because there is no diversity at the decision-making levels.

Maybe that is why characters such as Donald Trump continue to laugh in the face of genuine outrage and upset. Because everyone around him is joining in with the chorus of laughter. While the world wept with the daughter of George Floyd, Donald Trump took to Twitter to make his position on the matter clear. Trump tweeted: 'When the looting starts, the shooting starts.' Can you imagine becoming so comfortable with shooting, and death, and murder, and the killing of black people, that you tweet something like this? As the leader of the supposed free world, the lack of consideration and sheer bigotry really amazes me. The tweet wasn't only harmful because he referred to protesters as 'thugs', despite the police being the ones who were killing people unlawfully. The tweet became increasingly hurtful when the root of the quote was sourced. These words were first said by Eugene 'Bull' Connor, a segregationist who directed the use of police dogs and fire hoses against black demonstrators during the civil rights era. This is who Donald Trump quoted. This is who he showed agreement with. The tweet was deleted, but the damage had been done. An informal go-ahead was given to the riot police to adopt unruly behaviour.

In the days that followed, we saw innocent women being dragged from their cars and tasered in the street for absolutely no reason. We saw the police shoot unarmed, unthreatening protesters from an illegal point-blank range with rubber bullets, causing major injuries, including blindness in a few enraging cases. We saw riot police vandalising water stands and strategically placing piles of bricks by shop windows to inspire people to throw them when antagonised. Time and time again, our 'leaders' show us what side of the battle they would rather be on. It's terrifying to know that those with the power and responsibility to serve and protect everybody can sometimes hate you just as much as some civilians who haven't fully grasped the simple, beautiful truth of humanity. That we are different shades of the exact same race. Until those in positions of power come to understand this, can we ever feel safe? The poem 'Fearmongering' from Sophia Thakur's book *Somebody Give This Heart a Pen* explores one of the many repercussions of this historical, systemic pattern of racism:

Police aren't after conversations
they're after culprits.
They don't sharpen their fangs
for us to feel safe.
He wakes if he's lucky

with bite marks lining his back branding his black
with empty court dates and arrests made in vain.
Anything to sow shame
Anything to make sure he never feels safe.
So of course I ran
I've read this story 100 times over.
And I'd rather run blissful in ignorance
But alive,
when stopping could be suicide.

People think that the UK has grasped this idea of equality. That racism isn't as rampant here as it is in the US. That we are a more inclusive society. I admit that our numbers pale in comparison to the number of racially charged tragedies in the US, but it's near impossible to quantify structural racism. How do we attach figures to the number of children who leave their history lessons with an inferiority complex that follows them through the years like a dark shadow chained to their ankles? How do we measure imposter syndrome and micro-aggressions in the office? Racism in the UK is a raging whisper that travels through the veins of our very structure. It's less overt, so perhaps harder to identify. This is why people assume that activists in the UK are overreacting when we speak about racism. People see diverse billboards on the Underground and thriving

Indian students, and assume that the contentions of race have been solved.

Unfortunately, the only thing that the contentions have been is secretive. As much as I didn't want to make this an academic study of blackness in the UK, sometimes all we have are the statistics. And these are frightening. My children and grandchildren, the next part of this letter is possibly the most distressing. For that reason, it might also be the most important.

To begin, I'll outline the mission statement from the Metropolitan Police force. We cannot say that they are carrying out their job incorrectly until we have outlined the standard they have committed themselves to. Every police officer in England and Wales is bound to a code of ethics. The code was compiled by the College of Policing in its role as the professional body for policing. It 'sets and defines the exemplary standards of behaviour for everyone who works in policing'. Each employee is bound to ten standards of professional behaviour. The first of which is 'honesty and integrity'. In the code of ethics, this is the description attached to this clause: 'I will be honest and act with integrity at all times, and will not compromise or abuse my position.' There is nothing honest about and no integrity in the disproportionate number of black or brown stop-and-search victims in the UK. There is nothing honest about and no integrity in the number of black men who are wrongfully profiled because they 'resemble the suspect'. Of the many times I have been stopped, once it was because the officer was looking for a five-foot-one light-skinned male. I am a six-foot-one dark-skinned male. Just the other day, a key worker from the 4Front Project was illegally handcuffed, physically abused and detained by four police officers. The 4Front Project helps young people born into a disadvantaged community to get legal and tangible support after being arrested. The irony of it all is a piercing reminder that, to police officers, you could literally be Superman, but heaven help you if the face of Superman is black. Black men in the UK are forty times more likely than white men to be stopped and searched. Less than 16 per cent of these stops result in arrest, yet over 20 per cent result in verbal and/or physical violence from the police towards the innocent man. There is nothing honest about this.

The second point in the police's code of conduct claims that officers will 'act with self-control and tolerance, treating members of the public and colleagues with respect and courtesy'. The third promises that they will 'act with fairness and impartiality [and]not discriminate unlawfully or unfairly'. Trevor Smith was a fifty-two-year-old driver who lived in and loved Birmingham. He was well known in his community. On 15 March 2019, while Trevor was in bed in his flat, armed officers broke in and one of them shot him. Trevor never woke up. The investigation is ongoing and it is still unclear as to whether the police officer responsible will be charged with the killing or unjustified use of force against an unarmed person. At what stage does man in his own bed become a threat? Once the light from outside catches his melanin? Or as he turns over to expose his skin colour and unknowingly face a loaded gun?

The fourth point in the code of conduct instructs that officers should 'only use force to the extent that it is necessary, proportionate and reasonable in all the circumstances'. I struggle to understand where reason comes into play here. One case that I struggle to forgive is the murder of Stephen Lawrence.

I was with his brother on a panel discussion the other day and the strength of that family is unfathomable considering how unforgiving the past twenty-seven years have been towards them. In 1993, eighteen-year-old Stephen Lawrence was stabbed to death in London by a gang of white boys as he waited for the bus. The following day the names of all the boys were left in a telephone box close to the murder scene. The boys were all investigated and found not guilty. For years, in trial after trial, the judge told the Lawrence family that there was not enough evidence to arrest anyone. Stephen Lawrence's parents had to bury their child, who had been stabbed repeatedly, without the peace of justice. I can only imagine the rage they would have felt, while being unable to express it due to the undercover police officers, covert operations and mass press coverage surrounding the case. In 2007, after years of fighting for justice, it was announced that a new piece of evidence was being investigated. Except it wasn't new. It was as old as the case itself. A trace of Stephen Lawrence's blood was found on the clothing of one of the white boys. The case reopened and two of the boys (now men) were found guilty in 2012 and sent to jail. This is only a fraction of the justice that needed to be served. The entire case was riddled with deceit, police lies and the mishandling of evidence. Not much has changed since.

Point five of the code reads: 'I will, as a police officer, give and carry out lawful orders only, and will abide by Police Regulations.' There is a sick and infuriating culture of rape, sexual violence and abuse of power against female victims in the police force. This matter is spoken about significantly less than others, and I can understand why. It invalidates the entire force. But then the entire corrupt force needs invalidating if you ask me. Over the past ten years there have been hundreds of cases involving police officers who have abused their powers to rape, sexually assault or harass women and girls. I have never seen a single case catch the headlines. Between 2012 and 2018, PC Richard Hosken-Johns would take 'refreshment breaks' while on duty to visit two women who had reached out to the police for help. One of these women was suffering from domestic violence in her own home. He would sleep with them and then threaten them. Once this all came to light, he requested that both women lie about his relations with them. Where do you turn to if those who are paid to protect you could end up abusing you while you are most vulnerable? Debaleena Dasgupta is a lawyer who represents women who have been sexually assaulted and raped by police officers. She has said that she doesn't think 'any [victims] are quite as damaged as those who are victims of police officers'.

Point number six on the code of conduct surrounds ideas on confidentiality and treating information with respect and secrecy where necessary. Just a few weeks ago a picture of two dead black women found stabbed to death in a park was sent to a group chat by the police officers who had found the bodies. One of the photos is said to be a selfie with the corpses of the young women while still at the scene of the crime. I will not say any more on this because, honestly … what is there to say? The dehumanisation of black people stretches into every area of police activity, from arrests made in vain, all the way up to their death. Sandra Bland, a woman who was found hanging in her jail cell after being arrested for not signalling a lane change. An act that should never lead to being held in a prison or death. There is no humanity left in such behaviour. The lack of consideration is something that I have experienced myself for years. I've always said that I don't have a problem with the act of stop-and-search, provided there is reasonable suspicion. My problem is with how it is carried out. On numerous occasions I have been embarrassed for no good reason. Some of my friends have been stopped and searched while in their suits and with other people. If only the police officers showed the slightest bit of empathy in these scenarios. A simple reading of my rights or just letting me know why they are conducting the search would make a big difference. Instead, I'm treated like a criminal with no charges against me.

All of this makes we wonder who the police are hiring. Are they hiring racists who are eager to exercise their new power? Or does the police force make a good person go bad? In the US there is an inextricable link between the racist KKK group and law enforcement. In the US, KKK members are encouraged to 'avoid overt displays of their beliefs to blend into society and covertly advance white supremacist causes'. And many members of the force, who hold some of the highest positions of power, also belong to the KKK or affiliated racist groups. That is America. These are the people holding power. This is the UK. This is what we deny even existing, but I do wonder whether such is the case here, too. I can empathise with those who want to defund the police. We are paying to be killed. To be discriminated against. To be unfairly arrested. To be spat on, raped, criminalised and not given a fair trial. This is what our taxes go towards. It's not like we get a tax holiday every year in return for this service that works against black people. No. We serve them in our complicity. With our hands up and hoods down, we try to look as innocent as we actually are. Forgetting sometimes that our skin is seen as a weapon.

And when it isn't our skin, it's what our skin does. What I mean by that is that our behaviour is criminalised to a much higher degree than our white counterparts. There are so many young men who are serving unjustifiable sentences in prison for being found with a bag of weed. Yet the City of London is packed with cocaine-snorting professionals. The recent candidate for London Mayor has just announced that he thinks that 'companies should conduct random drug tests on their employees to stamp out middle-class cocaine use'. He went on to say that 'polite' drug use by professionals has led to the deaths of young black men on the streets of the capital. In 2010, according to a report published by *Release*, it was revealed that black people were 50 per cent less likely than white people to use drugs, but six times more likely to be stopped and searched for drugs. In the same year, the police charged 44 per cent of white people who were found with cocaine. They charged 78 per cent of black people. I agree that in some cases drug users should be charged, but equally, and in proportion to the drug that they have been using. Sometimes what they need is to be helped, not thrown into confinement.

Black people are jailed at six times the rate of white people for the same drug offences. How is that the least bit fair? Shouldn't the court have one rule for everybody? The policing of drug-possession offences is to the disadvantage of black and minority communities more than any other group. This can have a serious impact on a young black person's future career and prospects, in a way that cocaine done at the office work party will never have on our white counterparts. I do not condone smoking. Or any kind of drug use. But I can never understand why weed is so heavily criminalised in comparison to far more dangerous drugs – like alcohol, for example. I've grown up seeing drunk people passed out on the street, vandalising public property, hurling abuse at strangers, touching women inappropriately and then being helped into a cab by a police officer and sent home. A black boy only has to *look* like he could have drugs on him and he could be arrested, let alone be caught smoking. He could face up to five years if the judge is having a racist day. I've never smoked, but as far as I've seen, marijuana mellows the mind and encourages introspection. This is why it is being legalised in so many places. I see videos of all-white companies building new, legal weed empires across America. They are being endorsed and fully funded. Yet there are young men serving five- to ten-year prison sentences for carrying the tiniest bit of weed. On Twitter they reply to the posts that celebrate new marijuana mums with the hashtag '*FREE THE MANDEM*'. I agree; if it is legalised, free the mandem indeed. It seems as though the drugs that are used in the black community are far more heavily criminalised than those more common to white culture, like alcohol and cocaine, despite the impact of the latter being far worse.

The judge doesn't stop his or her discrimination at drugs, however. Unfortunately, the entire prosecution system favours white people over every other race. This happens every single day in the US, but I'll focus on how this plays out in the UK. White offenders have had a consistently lower average custodial sentence length for indictable offences than all other ethnic groups since 2014. You might be thinking, *Maybe fewer white people are guilty of crime.* The truth is that white defendants have consistently had the highest guilty plea rate since 2012, with 70 per cent pleading guilty in 2018. Defendants from mixed ethnic groups had a guilty plea rate of 64 per cent, black defendants had a rate of 57 per cent and Asian,

Chinese or 'Other' defendants had a rate of 56 per cent. This means that despite white people (at least the ones who are actually taken to court) being found guilty more than any other group, they are still arrested at a much lower rate than any other group. All this means is that, statistically, white people can get away with crime far more often than any other racial group. When I think about the number of accusations that Donald Trump, Prince Andrew and so many other high-profile white men have against them, I can hardly believe that the legal world turns a blind eye. As First Lady, Michelle Obama was scrutinised for the style of her dresses; Trump has had twenty-six allegations of sexual misconduct made against him and yet he somehow made the Oval Office. Multiple members of his friendship group have been proved guilty of abuse but faced little to no repercussions for their behaviour. It's a wicked world to be a victim in. Especially if your abuser is white and rich. This, along with so many other pockets of discrimination, is what led to the Black Lives Matter movement.

Personally, I do not support defunding the police. For me, this solves nothing. I do not want to end up with a lawless society. The idea of channelling some of the funding into our community to assist us in policing our young is a positive step, in my opinion. However, ultimately, policing is a job for the police. Police officers need to be retrained when it comes to interacting with the black community. They need to stop seeing us as a threat and approaching us as criminals in the first instance. I've been stopped numerous times in my life. I can distinctly remember one occasion that stands out. Why? Because the officer in question left an impression on me. He was courteous and approachable, as well as having an air of authority. He was different from the rest. We need officers like this. Officers who understand their oaths and truly believe they are here to serve the public. On top of that, individuals need to complete some level of psychoanalysis to ensure the police force is not employing anyone with hidden agendas. If you have one piece of rotten fruit in a basket, it eventually affects every fruit. The good becomes infected by the bad. I'll leave you with that thought.

I know I've spoken about the inception of the Black Lives Matter movement in an earlier letter to you, but I haven't shared my thoughts on what it has become. I recognise it as necessary and essential and it really has changed the world for the better. I know it is difficult for any social movement not to become a meme, a trend or a hashtag in 2020. Once that line has been crossed, it's near impossible to separate the real activist from those who just want to jump on a trend. I fear that this is what is becoming of the phrase 'Black Lives Matter'. That's what I feel it has become in some ways. A phrase, stripped of its meaning. The way in which the Black Lives Matter movement has been commercialised without action in some cases is evidence that black lives don't matter yet. Most of society still treats us as though we don't matter. We are looked at as suspicious before we've done anything. We are held in low esteem. We are judged. Not by the content of our character, as Martin Luther King Jr said, but by the colour of our skin. Black has become synonymous with bad. Black Lives Matter, to me, means fixing the negative stereotypes that are printed onto me. At ground zero we have to fix

the more subtle micro-aggressions that we have to deal with on a day-to-day basis. That's how we can all play a simple part in making a huge difference. And I don't know if the phrase Black Lives Matter encourages those more delicate, nuanced, incremental changes that we need in order to stop racism from being normalised.

When you hear 'Black Lives Matter', are you really thinking about the words themselves? BLACK LIVES MATTER. Black people matter. People of African heritage matter. Black folk matter. Darker skin matters. Equality of opportunity matters. Fair trials matter. Decolonising the curriculum matters. Natural hair matters. Youth centres matter. You don't think that, do you? You think of the movement, not the sentiment that started it. And that worries me a bit. It can take away from the initial statement. In some ways it has become a project without a plan. A statement or hashtag that starts and stops with the phrase.

This is of course not the case for everybody. I know that those close to the core of the cause are fighting the good fight every single day. I just worry. Social media has a tendency to trivialise almost everything. But perhaps movements need people to just jump on the trend to push it along. Even if their hearts aren't in it. Perhaps it's a numbers game. So whether you came to the protest to take black-and-white pictures in the hope of getting 'likes' or ending up in a textbook, or if you came just to say that you did ... maybe what matters most are the numbers. The display of unity. The camaraderie. Just maybe. But if I'm being completely honest – which is all I hope to be in this letter – the phrase has started to unsettle me. Black Lives Matter. Of course they do. Why, in 2020, do we need to have our throats burn with this phrase? What does that say of society? We are not even at a stage where we can say 'give us equal rights'. We are simply asking to *matter*. To be regarded as humans. Not to be shot, or hung from trees, or killed in our sleep, or refused jobs. We are just asking to matter.

Beyoncé just released a film on Disney+ called *Black Is King*. It explores blackness in a beautiful, empowering and authentic way. I did not grow up watching things like this. I grew up watching things that reinforced the idea that black lives didn't matter as much as white lives. So perhaps that is how we should revise the phrase. Maybe we should say, 'Black lives also matter.' Maybe then we won't be met with people screaming, 'But all lives matter.' Or maybe, in true Beyoncé fashion, we just have to take the mattering into our own hands as best we can. Sure, between you, my own children and our direct community, we can't force the hand of a judge to be fair, but maybe my generation can support yours in your areas of study. Maybe we can be mentors or share the real history of Africa with you. Maybe we have to become empowered ourselves in order to inspire change. I'm sure this is a crucial part of any historic revolution.

CHAPTER 8

THE LAST GENERATION TO MESS WITH

'Blackness has become the source of pride that it always should have been.'

know that we have done some heavy lifting in this letter. If I had the power to get into your mind as you read through the statistics, harsh realities and horror stories, I would. If only to tell you that, despite it all, I still believe in humanity. I still believe in better. In hope. In trying. Kendal, Sidéna, grandchildren, as you read this you may be at an age when I can no longer tell you what to do. If this is the case, you must know that on more than one occasion I have buried my head in my hands and asked the air, 'How am I ever going to get this right?' – a common moment among parent figures when we read a report card or drive home from a parent–teacher meeting and wonder whether our children will ever become what we hope. Sometimes I'm not even talking about you securing your dream job or giving me more grandchildren and great-grandchildren. Sometimes I wonder whether you will ever wash the plates in the sink without being told. Often it is the little things you don't do that tickle the helpless bones in my body. I ask myself, in a chorus with the other parents of the world, 'Why don't they just get it?' Why isn't it obvious that you should take your muddy shoes off at the door before walking on cream carpets? Why isn't it obvious that after a day of swallowing sweets like water, you should brush your teeth before bed? Why don't you want these things for yourself? If you know that fast food will damage your insides, and fruit will make you stronger and smarter, and you genuinely want to be both of these things, why don't you just eat healthily? These 'whys' are as familiar to parents across the world as is the conclusion we sometimes find ourselves coming to: 'Fine.' The universal translation for, 'It's easier to leave you to your own devices than it is to battle with you.' The 'fine' can sometimes manifest in the form of a sigh, the rolling of eyes or the waving of a hand that says, 'Go on then.' Sometimes it is easier to let you learn from your own mistakes than it is to convince you of the repercussions that could trail after your actions.

Sometimes. The only time a parent really does leave a child to their own devices is when they are sure it will not bring any real harm to the child. I'm yet to see a parent grow tired of wrestling for their child's hand on the side of a busy road. I don't think I've ever seen a parent let their child learn that lesson the hard way. They could die.

And this is why I write this letter: in the faith that we can learn from our mistakes, because people have in fact died for lack of lesson learning.

Collectively, we have already been left to run across the road and we have all been hit by cars. We have died over and over again. Some of us on boats crossing the transatlantic ocean. Some of us in the cotton fields. Some of us die every day in the office, laughing at racist jokes. Some of us die in the classroom, reading about the period of empire. We die until the lesson is learnt. At any given point, one person's racist joke is happening at the same time as a police officer is killing an innocent black man, or a judge is sentencing the wrong person to life imprisonment. We should be learning our lessons. We need to be. Luckily, the difference between running across a road and being hit by a car and reading this letter is that the latter exposes the opportunity for a better tomorrow. No matter how many times my mum had to tell me to behave as a child, no matter how many times I did not listen, she did not give up. Because what was more important than her growing fatigue was her hope for change. Her need for it. She had seen and heard of young boys being killed for nothing, and death was far too expensive a price to pay. For as long as we have air in our lungs, we have a chance to straighten out our children if they are going astray. There is an energy reserve deep in the anatomy of the parental being that never runs dry. I believe that we should invite the same energy reserve into all our bodies and tailor it towards improving humanity. Instead of going to more funerals, we should protest to prevent the next one. Instead of watching our children grow to be insecure about our blackness, we should empower you. To sew love back into the lessons of life.

This part of my letter is called 'The Last Generation to Mess With' – it initially had another word in place of 'mess', but for as long as I can protect your innocence, I must. I refuse to normalise the use of profanity in areas of purity. After studying the statistics and becoming infuriated over the figures, my desire to nourish and pour an abundance of goodness into you has overflown. This worries me, because I know I cannot protect you forever. I can hardly protect you from the world that social media opens you up to today, underneath my very roof. Social media has changed a lot of things for us parents. Suddenly we can only protect you to a certain degree. I might want to keep your eyes away from nudity, sexuality, violence and even just strangers, but with your fingertips you can arrive at any of these places within seconds. It's kind of like a sick magic carpet that pulls you into a whole other world, away from the safe one we try to build for you as parents. What's worse is that, just like Aladdin's carpet, you sometimes prefer the world away from ours. I guess it's easier to become the you of your imagination when behind a screen and not in front of a mirror. Perhaps if we all turned our phones off more often, we would catch our own reflections instead of this perception of ourselves that we try to create. I suppose it's more attractive to spend time in the world you get to mould with your own hands. Kendal and Sidéna would spend every hour of the day playing *The Sims* or Roblox if I let them. During this lockdown, with the sports centres and gyms closed, I've had a glimpse of how lazy they could become. It was frightening at first. To think that these are the children who might have to carry the revolution into the future. The same children I have to do battle with to get them to do some studying instead of watching Netflix all day. When did the worlds behind screens become more addictive than the one that gives us air to breathe? I suppose that is the exact aim of social media and streaming sites. To become addictive. To become necessary. To become a bigger part of our lives than our actual in-the-flesh lives.

I do wonder what my own grandparents would say if they read this letter. If they saw how broken the world still is. And then went on TikTok to see what the children are investing their time in. I'm sure they would roll over in their graves. Social media has made us all a bit softer than we can afford to be. It's big and entertaining enough to distract us from what happens outside of our window. We sit in restaurants with racist owners, but we don't ever think about that. Instead we pick places where we can take pretty pictures for Instagram. We Snapchat our food while it gets cold. I'm not sure that my grandparents could even afford to turn a blind eye to inequality. It was quite literally on their doorstep. They could not scroll past it. They couldn't put a filter on it. They couldn't care about it only for as long as it takes to like a photo and move on. There was nothing to distract them from the harsh realities of race. Maybe that is why they were so much stronger than we are. And so much stronger than my own children and grandchildren are likely to be.

Perhaps we assimilate into our context, and theirs demanded a thicker skin, while this generation are more concerned with clear skin. I guess I would be, too, if my Instagram feed was full of unattainable standards of perfection. There are nineteen-year-olds saving up their student-loan money to fly to Turkey to get BBL (Brazilian butt lift) surgery. Young women are getting hip fillers and breast implants before they're twenty years old. Before their bodies have even finished developing. It breaks my heart to see how much pressure social media has put on people, especially young women. I read a poem from Sophia Thakur called 'Fairground Lenses' that I do feel really sums up the Instagram generation:

My body was once better than comparison
but other images of beauty have long stained my eyes
and I can't help but plaster potential over every part of
    me,
and see much of my anatomy as space to rectify,
forgetting how it felt to look myself up and down
and be at the very least,
satisfied

The wrong things are given the utmost importance. When I talk to the women in my life I try to remind them that they are beautiful regardless of whether anybody says so. That they are perfectly made. That their laugh lights up a room. That their charisma is addictive and their character charming. We have to empower each other to fall in love with real life. With the real us. One day, somebody could finally create a virus that will shut down the Internet. We have to be at a point as a people where, if this happens, our sense of self-worth isn't shut down with it. We need to ensure that our mental health is stable enough to be able to exist beyond our online world. Beyond the distraction of a phone. We need to be able to stand in front of the mirror, naked, without the thought of somebody else's body, somebody else's bathroom and somebody else's life intruding on our reality. I'm probably showing my age here. I don't know many grandparents who massively love social media. It's just such a foreign concept to us. The fact that influencers have taken over the traditional role of brand marketing – and from the comfort of their bedrooms – is insane. The incredible kind of insane.

The younger generation have taken the concept of *The Sims* or Habbo and applied it to real life. They have created an entirely new world, with new social circles and communities within it. The line between fact and fiction has been blurred to the point of not existing. Thanks to the globalisation of the Internet, they can create groups with people from all over the world and connect with like-minded people that they would never have had the opportunity to meet otherwise. How they have built themselves empires that offer services and even generate income can only be called impressive. My two eldest children both run online businesses. My son has his own fashion brand and my eldest daughter has her own online clothing boutique. Yes, my grandparents were perhaps mentally stronger than my two youngest daughters, but they did not have the innovation or confidence to do what I see being done today. Especially during the coronavirus lockdown period. I was online more than ever and I saw black creativity, cohesion and intelligence take over the Internet. To the point where huge brands were begging to get involved with these black content creators, who were shifting the world and keeping us all entertained during a global pandemic from their parents' homes.

It was remarkable to witness. There was a radio station called No Signal that, for weeks at a time, hosted radio clashes between popular artists. It was set up by a young man named Jojo, who had also set up an events company called Recess, which put on sold-out events catered to the black community. The weekend he decided to set up the station was the weekend he was meant to host a sold-out event at Village Underground in East London. After coronavirus meant that he had to cancel the event, he asked himself, what can we do with our resources, this new attention with everyone now online, something for our own people? The first weekend, 300 people tuned in using the hashtag #NS10v10. Today, Spotify have made playlists from their show, they have had huge press coverage across mainstream media and they are still catering for the entertainment and empowerment of the black community. The live stream kept the entire Twitter and Instagram timeline entertained during one of the bleakest parts of any young person's life. Over 200,000 listeners tuned in to the clash between Wizkid and Vybz Kartel. The clash brought black communities across the world together. From London to Canada to Africa. Celebrities that had featured on the clash were even tuning in and showing support. Burna Boy, his mum and his girlfriend, rapper Stefflon Don, all tuned in and even called in at one point during the Burna Boy clash. In every sense of the term, No Signal had re-created 'black radio' using their parents' Wi-Fi. This generation of young black people are seeing where mainstream society has neglected to cater for black people, and they are beginning to do it themselves. Not just in music, but across the board.

Tobi Kyeremateng is a theatre producer who recognised the racial disparities that existed in that space. You could have an all-black theatre cast and not a single black audience member. This is due to a range of socioeconomic reasons, from the price of tickets to how shows are marketed. Having worked in theatre, Tobi recognised how important it was for young black children to be exposed to the art form, so she created an initiative called the Black Ticket Project. Among many other amazing things, they pay for students from disadvantaged backgrounds to attend artistic cultural events. They bridge the gap between youth workers, schools, charities and cultural institutions to ensure that every child has an opportunity to engage in the arts. Just recently they announced that they are dedicating £5,000 to young black people from low-wage economic backgrounds who need to appeal their A-level results. And might I add, Tobi, the founder, is twenty-five years old. She has done more for disadvantaged black communities than some politicians who are paid to do this. The same can be said for the rapper Stormzy and footballer Marcus Rashford. Following the Black Lives Matter protests, Stormzy pledged to donate £10 million to UK organisations that seek to tackle racial inequality. And when our Tory government decided not to extend free school meal vouchers to the summer holidays, which would dispro-portionately affect children from poorer backgrounds whose parents literally rely on this very standard offering, Marcus Rashford stepped up. The Manchester United star wrote an impassioned letter to MPs, pointing out that he, like millions of other children, relied on free school meals as a child. He then went on to raise £20 million to supply three million meals to vulnerable people during the lock-down. In his letter to MPs he wrote, 'This is not about politics, it's about humanity.' His plea was heard and the decision was reversed.

In every area of the black experience, there is a young person deciding to serve their own community in the way that the government serves the white community. It's a shame that we are neglected in so many areas of concern, but I do have faith in the bravery and forward thinking of this next generation. They have really taken to this ancient African idea of *Ubuntu*. This Zulu word means 'human-ity'. The principle is that '*I am because you are*'. It stems from the same African school of thought that pushed me and my boys to the protest that Saturday. The idea that it takes a village to raise and protect a child. I think it is only natural to want to develop your own community. Especially in the face of such oppression. A beautiful example of this was the rebirth of Black Pound Day. A day when everybody buys from black businesses. On social media, there were threads on black-owned soaps, hair products, food, furniture, candles and just about everything else we wouldn't usually buy from a black-owned retailer. The idea is that, within other ethnic groups, wealth is raised by their own community, but in the black community there has always been a culture of outsourcing to other groups for our supplies. The majority of hair shops are owned by Indians. Our gyms are owned by Jewish people. Our nail technicians are Chinese. If we need a poster done or a business card made, we go to Moonpig, when all the while the talent exists in our own community to do all of these things.

It wasn't until these protests happened and the Black Lives Matter movement became ten times more vocal that I began to see people speak about blackness so openly and without fear.

Sometimes it felt like a swear word that we would tiptoe around, hoping not to offend anybody. Over the space of a few weeks, it became perfectly okay to say the word BLACK. To call out CEOs on how many BLACK employees they had in their companies, which benefited from BLACK culture. The label of blackness was finally being revealed in every space, and it was such a breath of fresh air to see it attached to progressive projects and a level of confidence I had never seen before.

That's another thing I must give to the younger generation. There is something about starting their own businesses that has allowed them to be both soft and strong at the same time. They are not scared. They are informed. Far more informed than my grandparents could have been before the age of the Internet. They ruffle feathers, pull out facts, demand change and hold people to account. They are far more unapologetic than we were as children. A hundred times more unapologetic than my grandparents were. My mum and grandparents were more submissive and scared to speak out. I imagine it was because the cost of speaking out was far greater then than it is now. Today, it is even encouraged to a degree. In my grandparents' day, they needed the jobs that oppressed them. They relied on that money to survive. Speaking out against injustice could have meant they were attacked in the street, fired, bullied or even killed. They were demure because they had to be. Not all of them, of course. The generations before us also set fire to court houses and staged boycotts and hunger fasts for weeks on end. I'm not even sure if this new generation would go as far as to collectively put their lives on the line for a cause. I'm thankful that that isn't such a necessity now. I'm grateful that young men are making enough money to stitch themselves back into their communities, and that young women are confident enough in their heritage to teach younger girls how to love and take care of their hair. This is something that was lacking when I grew up.

As part of being apologetic about our blackness, we would sometimes conceal parts of it where we could. There wasn't as much celebration surrounding blackness as there is today. Especially not when it came to young women and their hair. It was the age of relaxing creams and hot combs. 'Neat' was synonymous with straight. 'Good hair' meant as close to European hair as possible. We would never see women on TV or posters with Afro hair. Even the few black Barbie dolls I remember my cousins having had long, straight hair. The only time we would see coarse, Afro-Caribbean hair was on TV adverts asking for donations for Africa. For so long our standard of beauty has been attached to whiteness or European features, but it really does feel like it's changing. In some ways it's done a complete U-turn. Now everybody wants a spray tan and women are getting more lip fillers and butt implants to copy black features. Today there are one million YouTube channels run by black women, talking about how to take care of natural hair.

I'm seeing all hair textures on the cover of mainstream magazines and adverts. That never would have happened even ten years ago. I look at my daughters and grand-daughters and see nothing but beauty. I hope the world never tries to convince them otherwise. There is a sense of black pride that has arisen over the past few years that I pray continues.

In school, I remember that Africans would deny being from Africa. The only time they would admit to being African was if they pretended to be related to a footballer. That's one thing that was never taken away from Africans.

My youngest daughters, Sidéna and Kendal.

They had fantastic football teams that would almost always qualify for the World Cup. I remember how the World Cup season used to draw out the Nigerian, Ghanaian, Ivorian, Cameroonian and Senegalese boys in school. They had that over us West Indians. Football wasn't our sport per se. That being said, it was still generally cooler to be from the Caribbean. Perhaps it was because our music was more popular, and most of the slang that all of the children spoke came from the Island. It was cool to be Jamaican. That was the only avenue for being proud to be black. Africa got a really bad press growing up. The other students genuinely believed that the entire continent of Africa was one big village with no food, money or resources. With flies everywhere and no infrastructure. People thought that the food African students would bring in was smelly, so it must have been cheap. In fact, many people still do today. When I talk about the stadiums, luxury villas, state-of-the-art architecture, schooling, shopping malls, beach houses, resorts, music studios and aesthetically amazing places of worship in Africa, people are always shocked. It's remarkable to think that even after the birth of social media, the media can still limit the mind of man to its own echo-chamber reality. Recently, however, I've witnessed a beautiful transition from hiding to celebrating Africa. Afrobeat has become one of the most-played music genres in the world, and West Africa has become a popular tourist destination. In 2018 and 2019, Ghana hosted a 'Homecoming'. American celebrities who had never been in touch with their roots all made their way to the coast and were amazed by how developed and luxurious West Africa was. It has become the place of pride that it always should have been. Blackness has become the source of pride that it always should have been. When I see you all eating your traditional food, singing along to reggae, it breaks my heart to think that there are things and people in society who will try to stop you from celebrating yourselves. If the world won't help you, I must. The future relies on your self-confidence.

CHAPTER 9

UTCAI

'We want to give the youth something better to do.
Give them someone better to become.'

imagine that by the time you read this letter, UTCAI will be a familiar phrase in your life. I hope that in all its familiarity, the nucleus of the organisation remains the same. UTCAI stands for United to Change and Inspire. That's exactly what we hope to do. To highlight societal problems that keep marginalised groups at a disadvantage and help remedy the wounds. We solidified our brotherhood after the protest that day. Something about connecting our cords and moving as a team was so empowering. As people, we are stronger together. I truly believe in the saying 'No man is an island'. That's not to say that loneliness is the most compassionate of monsters. Sometimes life strips us of everything and everyone to strengthen us.

The beauty of unity is that we don't have to be *as* strong if other people are there to contribute their own strength. This is something we kept at the forefront of

From left to right – UTCAI: Chris Otokito, me, Lee Russell
and Jamaine Facey.

our minds on the thirteenth day of the sixth month of
the year 2020.

We all work in the world of fitness or fighting and we
all had combat experience, whether it be in a ring, in a
cage, on a mat or in the street. Our reasonable service
was to our community. What drove us to the protest on
that unsuspecting Saturday continues to drive us today.
We came together as concerned parents, as elders with
children who looked just like the children we'd been
seeing on television protesting and hoping with all their
heart that their voice and presence would make the

difference needed to transform the story. As we walked through the streets of London with capes of responsibility wrapped around our shoulders, we were looking out for our sons and daughters. Our mothers and fathers. Everyone who shares the same melanin and has therefore become a target. It's a shame that oppression can be so uniting. I know the saying goes 'Misery loves company', but sometimes I think misery *needs* company. The world is far too heavy to carry on one set of shoulders. The future generation is far too precious for us all not to try to protect. We are underpinned by the African proverb that reminds us that it does take a village to raise a child. To raise a child, you must first ensure that they are kept alive. And as the mortality of black skin was the very reason people were taking to the streets that day, we had to ensure that we did not fall at the first hurdle. Survival.

The five of us went to Waterloo thinking that if we can ensure that black lives are not taken, hopefully somebody else at some point can ensure that black lives can be improved. Hopefully, if we can defuse the violence, the violence will not make the headlines and thus impede all the positive change that has been happening. It felt like a duty to stand between our youth and any harm that may seek to implicate or violate them and their future. We didn't just want to protect the black mothers and children from the white opposition, we needed to protect the future from bad press. Unfortunately, one headline can destroy a movement. Well … if the movement is aiming to empower black people.

Together, the boys and I changed the narrative. We contributed a counter-headline to the ones the media has been pushing for years. The perception of black men as violent, angry and abusive. Unluckily for those who strive to perpetuate this perception, none of these labels could have been attached to the video of five men saving a white man's life. On that day, even if only for a moment, we hijacked the usual narrative and spun it on its head. I like to think that we stopped Monday morning's headline from reading 'Father of three and ex-policeman is killed by black youths at the Black Lives Matter protest'. There would be no mention of his racist behaviour. There would be no memory of the very reason why he travelled miles to attend an anti-black protest. All that the media would have had the world remember is that a white man was killed by angry black people. The entire story of the victim is often only reserved for black or other minorities death. After George Floyd was killed, some news channels began circulating stories about his past transgressions from his youth. As if staying alive is something that has to be earned if you are not white. To live is to exercise our birth right.

We created UTCAI to add value to the years that everybody lives on this side of eternity. Together, the boys and I want to champion equality in our community. Like an electric current, we want this agenda to grow beyond our minds, experiences and expertise. UTCAI will team up with like-minded people who are experts in each of the fields in which we hope to inspire change. We know that all of the groundwork we do in our own local community can only have a limited impact on the wider black experience across the country. To remedy this, we hope to take our research and revolution to Parliament, and impact on policy that can filter down into the communities that the four of us cannot tangibly reach. Not just yet, anyway. We are very fortunate to be mentored by one of the most prominent individuals in championing for change: Lord Dr Michael Hastings. Lord Hastings has been working tirelessly behind the scenes, in Parliament, in prisons, in youth centres and on the streets, for decades. We trust that his heart is aligned to the betterment of the black community, while his mind is well versed in the laws of the land. It takes multiple different minds and methods to change the world. UTCAI will focus on the few that we believe will really reshape the foundation of our world. We want to delve deep into the criminal justice system, education, mental health and youth development. We also plan to develop a corporate angle, where we can explore unconscious bias and discrimination in the workplace. Our main focus, however, is young people. Young people of all backgrounds but especially the impoverished, of which a large percentage are black.

In all of these areas, we aren't necessarily trying to reinvent the wheel or introduce a completely new vehicle for change. There are so many incredible people doing life-changing work in all of these areas. With this new platform we have been blessed with, we just want to align ourselves with some of the best of those people, shining a light in the process on the groundwork that is already being done by community leaders and activists. It can be so difficult to break into the public eye. Especially when you are doing something that will challenge those who hold privilege. This is why we felt obligated to set up this organisation. We realised that, since the day of the protest, we have a platform, and people from different backgrounds are keen and intrigued to know more about us. In this current climate, it would be a travesty not to put this attention to good use and play our part in fighting the good fight. We've been those guys sitting in front of the TV, frustrated with the world but not knowing what can be done to make more people open their eyes and do better. On the day we went out, we finally had something to do. It opened the door to making more of a tangible impact. We really do feel as though we can help bring about lasting change, provided the other players in the game are listened to as well.

For us, in many ways it begins with education. A lack of learning and empowerment at a young age is what leads to inferiority and superiority complexes. If we can fix it at the root, perhaps more people could come to define what is 'good' and 'bad' as something that goes beyond 'black' and white', and instead see that we all need to unite in our attempt to fix what is broken. Racism. Children are impressionable; they are susceptible to the behaviour they are exposed to. I know what some of the younger children in disadvantaged areas have grown up witnessing. Pauline and I were lucky to have cousins who lived quite close by, who were raised similar to us. We were influenced by Aunty Dell's children, our cousins Antoinette and Paul, in our early years. They shared similar standards and concepts of good and bad. If you come from a working-class background, the chances are you will have to be babysat at some point because your parents have to work. If we didn't have Aunty Dell, Uncle Charles and the rest of our extended family to go to for support, we would have become inspired by the wrong side of the street. Luckily, our entire family was big on education, but this isn't the case for all families.

If some children are never exposed to something different in real life, the bar they set for themselves hovers far too close to the reality of poverty. Getting good grades is currently the only window some children have to escape this dangerous cycle. That is why I have been so heartbroken recently at the handling of students who have had to miss exams due to the pandemic. As I write this, the estimated results for GCSE and A-levels have arrived. There is such a devastating uproar among students and parents who have just had their children's dreams of university and a better life stripped away by an algorithm that does not serve those from disadvantaged areas. The assessment criteria used the past achievement data from schools to guess which grades each student in the new academic year might achieve. This does not account for the ability of the individual child. The child who stayed up late to work hard to go to a good university and see something different from the only life they've known. The students whose parents have spent the little money they have on tutors in the hope of a brighter future. This algorithm looks at the location of the school and the past grades and assumes that every child can be tarred with the same brush. This is exactly how the cycle continues. How the poor stay poor and the rich stay rich. Some students were predicted A*s by teachers who have known and supported them. On results day, they open their letters to see that the computer has decided they will not excel beyond their surroundings. The computer gives the student Bs and Cs. This student gets rejected from the University of Oxford, for no other reason than where she is from. This is just another form of prejudice and discrimination. It breaks my heart because good grades really are all that some students have to build the life they desire.

This has disproportionately affected those from under-privileged backgrounds. Those who may not be able to afford to resit the exams that they never took in the first place. I hope that by the time this letter is opened and read, something would have been done to make amends. I know that they are considering a U-turn on the decision, but it will still affect students whose original, preferred universities are now full.

Having our children go to schools in underprivileged areas because that is demographically where we have been placed has plagued us since our arrival on these shores. Mortgages and the price of living have been systematically structured to keep black people out of more affluent areas. Most Caribbean people in the sixties and seventies lived in Notting Hill Gate, Battersea, Clapham, Brixton or Hackney. Over the years, the price of just about everything was raised. Given how rife racism was back then, it was almost impossible for black people to get the jobs that would pay enough to allow them to continue living in these areas as they became

smarter. Most people's requests for mortgages were denied, and the rental prices got higher and higher. Black people were intentionally moved out of these areas into council estates in rougher areas. Only the few who managed to buy property in those areas and never moved reap the benefits today of good schooling for their children. I believe they call this gentrification. I won't scare you with the price of houses in these areas today. Or the price of avocados.

Offering a new perspective and way of living to children in disadvantaged areas is paramount to building a stronger future for everybody. Not just black children. I've lived in London for the majority of my life, and if there's one thing I can be sure of, it's that race isn't the only dividing line that determines the distribution of resources. Britain thrives in the space of class discrimination, too. The white underclass also faces major disenfranchisement, neglect and prejudice. Schools in low-income, majority-white areas struggle to supply basic resources such as textbooks for every child, while schools in more affluent areas are able to equip children with iPads and extra learning resources. If the seeds are unequally distributed, no matter how much watering takes place, the gardens will never be level. In schools we hope to work on planting seeds of inspiration, motivation and opportunity for all children. Starting with my own. My younger children and you, my grandchildren, will receive all of my effort in trying to ensure that you experience as wholesome a childhood as possible.

We want to go into schools and possibly lead eight- to ten-week workshops. During those sessions we want to empower young people. Our angle is quite unique to schools. Usually, when a group of black men come into a class, they are telling the children to stay out of gangs and leave drugs alone. We want to teach them martial arts. Hopefully through the focus and discipline they will develop through one of the martial arts, they will naturally stay away from gangs and drugs. Learning martial arts instils discipline and mental strength. It increases the confidence of both adults and children. I've seen how physical empowerment can turn into mental empowerment, and the children need that. To compliment that mental stimulation, we have a vision of teaching children a more decolonised curriculum. I know this is something that is very, very slowly being rolled out in a very, very few schools, but we hope that once we expose the importance of a more wholesome history syllabus, the education boards will realise that it is time for an upgrade in all schools.

In fact, I hope upgrades are encouraged across the board. From the small things like micro-aggressions in school to the bigger things like reparation. The mention of repaying the countries that were ravaged during the slave trade is often met with shock. I can never understand why. Not only were these countries held hostage for 400 years, but in the process they were set back 400 years. That's 400 years less than the invading countries have had to grow wealth, to build up their communities, to farm resources and create institutions. Today, a number of universities and banks have traced their first financial backing to slave money. Once slavery was abolished, instead of financially sowing into the communities that were traumatised and destroyed for centuries, the wealthy slave owners passed on their money to their children, who went on to build establishments such as Lloyds

Bank, HSBC and a number of universities across the world. Between 10 and 20 per cent of Britain's wealth is inextricably linked to slavery. You might be wondering how on earth this happened. How the slave masters ended up with the upper hand, again. Well, in order to bring about the abolition of slavery, the country's leaders brought about an act called the Slave Compensation Act. It compensated no slaves, but rather the slave owners for the loss of their 'property' and business due to the criminalisation of slavery. Can you imagine that? The equivalent of billions of pounds in today's money was paid out to slave owners to cushion the fact that they could no longer kidnap, torture and dehumanise other humans. The leaders were so adamant that slave owners should be compensated for their loss that they had to take out loans so large that they were only paid off in 2015. Up until five years ago, some British people were still indirectly getting paid for the fact that their great-great-grandparents were once racist. On the other side of the world, countries that were pillaged by the slave trade are still going through recessions. Some owe endless amounts of money to the very countries that enslaved them and then forced them to take out huge loans to survive. Not only were people in Africa and the Caribbean at a disadvantage during slavery, they then had to watch the money they worked to put into white pockets go into cementing generational wealth and infrastructure that would continue to oppress them. I can't believe people say that these things don't run deep. It is wrong not to pay reparations. It is wrong to pick and choose which nations receive reparations. It is wrong to leave melanin-heavy nations out of this conversation. It is theft and it is not spoken about enough. We hope to bring a lot of harsh truths to the table, without passing blame, but instead commissioning change.

With the help of Lord Hastings, we also want to expose the inequalities of the criminal justice system. I won't go into the statistics again. I'm sure that if you've read this letter, you know exactly why something needs to be done in this area. It's not only about ensuring that law enforcers and judges are obeying the law, it is about ensuring that rehabilitation is made available for those who are already in prison. Unfairly and fairly. Only 9 per cent of the prison population in the UK get visits. Nine per cent. That means that 91 per cent of prisoners are cut off from society and have no communication with the outside world. How is anybody ever expected to come out and adjust to normal life after that? This is one of the reasons why the reoffending rate of prisoners is so high. They come out into what is sometimes an entirely new world, carrying the mental strain of years in isolation, with no helping hand to guide them back into 'civilised' society.

For some, the only way out of a troubled mind is through narcotics, and for others, they don't believe that they have any part to play in society, so they go straight back into the life that pushed them behind bars in the first place. We see the impact that low self-esteem can have on a student in a healthy environment. It can negatively impact on their willingness to try new things, make new friends or even push themselves to learn and work harder. For the average person, this mental block can become physical in many ways. Imagine what it must be like for somebody who has spent years in an actual physical prison and in mental isolation. There is a world of rebuilding to do inside the heart, mind and body of someone who has spent time in jail, if we ever hope to change their story.

To break that cycle, we need to ensure that rehabilitation is made a priority in the prison complex. Something as small as going into prisons and just talking about our feelings can have an incremental impact on somebody's life and mental health. Everything stems from the mind, and this is something that is not spoken about enough in the black community.

I can put my hands up and say that I'm still learning how to talk about it. Terms such as depression or PTSD were things we lived through as members of the diaspora but never thought to explore and learn about. Perhaps if we did, we wouldn't be a generation of broken adults. UTCAI wants to do a lot of work on issues of mental health. In our community, there is a reliance on drugs or suppression to survive the plight of being black. Research suggests that experiencing racism can be very stressful and have a negative effect on overall health and mental health. There is a growing body of research to suggest that those exposed to racism may be more likely to experience mental-health problems, such as psychosis and depression. Risk of psychosis in black Caribbean groups is estimated to be nearly seven times higher than in the white population. And black men are reported to have the highest rates of drug dependency of all ethnic groups. Young boys are turning to weed to sedate their anxieties or rage, before their brain has even fully developed, but the marijuana that is bought and sold today is often manufactured using damaging chemicals and can even be mixed with other addictive drugs. This has a lifelong impact on their cognitive development and leads to a reliance on substances. That is one hell of a trail and it needs to be broken. I believe that education and resources can ensure that this rollercoaster towards mental deterioration is understood, resolved and stopped with expert help.

In UTCAI, we are all fathers. Every single breath that we take comes from a heart that beats for our children and for you, our grandchildren, and other young people just like you. The development of our youth through projects, classes, mentoring sessions and organised training is key to keeping other parents' hearts at ease. There is nothing scarier than wondering if your child is out on the street getting caught up with the wrong group. We want to give the youth something better to do. Give them someone better to become.

CHAPTER 10

LEGACY

'Our children will carry the torch and continue to shine a light on inequality.'

care most about the opinions of my family and friends. The world could be watching, but how you, my children and grandchildren, see me is what matters most. Yours are the eyes in which I see myself. The weight of strangers' eyes hovers over my head constantly, but you children kiss me in the centre of my forehead and realign me to my 'why'. The most important roles that I have ever had in my life are the roles of father and grandfather. I'd like to think I have worn and continue to wear these robes well. I hope the world lets you remember me as such. Currently, I am confident that it will, but I know how the truth can be twisted with time. My nieces are teachers and heads of department in schools, and they have started sowing seeds into the curriculum that will protect my legacy. Children have already started studying me in schools and just recently I have been plastered onto a huge £5-note billboard in Peckham. I guess this is how a legacy is started. There is talk of turning me into a statue or giving me an MBE. This excites me just as much as it will excite you and my children. If you can open your textbooks one day and read about me and be proud, if you can point to my picture on the page and say that you share the same blood as this man, and do it with pride, then I will have done all that I set out to do in this life.

Not to be morbid, but on the day of my physical passing, when my body is lowered into the earth from which it came, I will know all that I need to know about the legacy I have left. I will watch my final judgement take place. Surrounded by the truth of the afterlife, I will look down from the sky and watch my family say goodbye. From how tightly they hug, from how frequently they cry, from the number of toasts and the depth of the speeches, I will know whether I have accomplished what I was put here to do. My funeral will be my final legacy. It will be the last page of my chapter on fatherhood and grandfatherhood. How the rest is written will be a testament to how well I wrote. And I hope that in all my efforts to expose how beautiful the world can be if we just let love be our guiding force, my offspring will mourn the dead, but fight like hell for the living. This is what we hope to do through UTCAI, and I hope that even when the founders pass away, our children will carry the torch and continue to shine a light on inequality just as Bernice

Albertine King does with the legacy of her own father, Martin Luther King Jr. There is something as sure as blood that makes me want to build something with and for my family. Before UTCAI, it was a book written with my brother on how we met and our family history. I'm sure we will write that book one day. I smile at the thought of how joyous it will be to sit together as a family and reminisce about old times. I hope that in nostalgia we will find men to be proud of. Men who did their part in the quest for justice.

The thing with fighting for equality is that although we fight with freedom in mind, I know that I will one day pass away, still in pursuit of a better tomorrow. In my time here on earth, the most I can hope to do is inspire. Inspire change, inspire unity and inspire my lineage. Inspire people to face their bias head on, and actually engage in a conversation with a black person, to learn that they were judging them incorrectly. Inspire white people to acknowledge their micro-aggressions and be more respectful to other cultures. Inspire communities to integrate with their neighbours and hopefully come to find how beautiful it is to engage in new cultures. Inspire colleagues to live up to the UK's title as a melting pot society, and embrace minority traditions every now and again. I hope to inspire other leaders to lead with fairness at the root of their decision making. I hope to inspire young men to step up and protect the younger generation. To inspire fathers to make a career of being positive, present role models to their children. I hope to inspire absolutely everybody to give a voice to the silent parts of them that have something to say about the need for institutional reform.

At this stage, I cannot be certain that it will be through TV interviews and radio discussions. In fact, I can only hope that this letter will inspire the ones who will go on to inspire the many. But I can hope. I hope that one day I get to write more books. One with my family, delving deeper into our Hollywood-worthy story, but also the first book I ever wanted to write, on the power of fitness. I hope that I get the chance to pull fitness into the mental-health and empowerment conversation as a vital element of wellbeing. I, like many fitness professionals, hope to create an app. But one that will go beyond steps and calorie counting. I want features that can track your sleeping patterns and your mental health. I'd want it to have a journaling and therapeutic element, with a live therapist that you could reach if necessary. If there is one thing that I've learnt as a black man, it is that when a mother cannot get through … when politics neglects … when teachers suspend and jobs overlook … sport often becomes the home away from home. The area in which we discover our strengths and our community. While writing this letter and running around London doing TV and magazine features, I've had to think about community a lot. I've had to find a sure reason to continue pursuing this cause. As a quiet, family-orientated man, I've had to really sit with the core reason to keep on pushing. And now, however many pages on, I think I've finally understood why I must. Because my children are watching. You, my children and grandchildren, are watching. And I can only hope that my life is an example of picking good each time. Of stepping into situations where a minority is at

Back row, left to right – Sidéna, Theo, Tyler and Dominic.
Front row, left to right - Kendal, Asia and Kyrie.

harm, and making my presence known. Of inspiring those around me to do the same. If ever you come across a man mishandling a woman, or a woman abusing a child, or a child bullying a classmate … I can only hope that you and those around you are inspired to step in and say no. I hope that any concept of safety that you develop includes the safety of the most vulnerable. I hope you come to learn nobody is ever equal unless everybody is. Nobody is ever safe unless everybody is. In a time where people would rather put their heads down, and phone cameras up … I hope you pull your voice from your toes up and speak out against what is wrong. It feels so simple. If enough people come together, the perpetrator becomes the minority, and the power they once held lessens.

I hope that you remember me as a fair and honest individual. As a man of integrity. I would like for you to think of me as a man who made a huge difference in the fight for equality. I truly believe that equality is attainable if we all work together. We are one race, the human race. Even those of you who are not directly affected by inequality but continue to live in an unfair society cannot continue to accept what is happening. You must call out racism in all walks of life and remain silent no more. Black people cannot continue to live a lesser life for no other reason than the colour of their skin. We cannot continue to exist in a constant state of attack. We cannot continue to convince the world that we deserve equality. Equality should exist at the core of humanity, and absolutely everybody should take part in balancing our world. It should not be black against white. It needs to be everyone versus racism.

All my love,
Your Dad and Grandad

ACKNOWLEDGEMENTS

I owe an enormous debt of gratitude to my mum. For everything you have done and continue to do for Pauline and me and for your loyalty and commitment in caring for Grandmum. Without your love, affection and guidance we would not be the well-rounded individuals we are today. I hope I've made you proud.

To Grandmum, for being a loving grandma. I have only fond memories of being with you in Coventry and Jamaica.

Nanny Millie, rest in peace; I have never forgotten you and I hope you're proud of me and Dominic.

Thank you to Uncle Charles and Oliver for being role models that I could look up to. Not having a dad was tough, but your presence gave me strength and confidence as a young boy. I'd also like Pauline Hutchinson, Donovan Hutchinson, Paula Hutchinson, Pamela Hutchinson, Toni Lewis, Juanita Smith, Pedro McLeod and Paul Miller to take a bow. Your tremendous support over the years has been invaluable.

Thank you to Raymond the barber. Because of you, I filled a void in my life which is now filled by the rest of my siblings.

The marvellous Sophia Thakur, working with you has been an absolute pleasure. From your writing style to your work ethic, you are a superstar in the making.

To the great team that have supported me on my new journey so far: Aaron, Keisha, Max and the team at 84 World.

Immense gratitude to Gita Bartlett for managing my PR during that frantic first four weeks. You were amazing.

HarperCollins, thank you for investing in me and giving me the platform to share my thoughts.

ABOUT THE AUTHOR

Patrick Hutchinson is a personal trainer and a children's athletics coach from South London who received worldwide attention after he was photographed carrying an injured counter-protestor to safety during a Black Lives Matter demonstration in central London. The photograph, which was taken by Dylan Martinez at a protest in response to the killing of George Floyd and in the midst of the COVID-19 pandemic, has been upheld as a defining moment of 2020 and the BLM movement. As a proud father-of-four and a grandfather-of-four, family is at the heart of everything for Patrick; if he isn't training you will find him taking care of his children and grandchildren, who are the most important things to him of all.

PICTURE CREDITS

p.22 © TKE

p.75 © Barcroft Media/Getty Images

p.90 Courtesy Massachusetts Institute of Technology Museum

p.94 © Ted S. Warren/AP/Shutterstock

p.125 © TKE

p.132 © George W. Hales/Stringer/Hulton Archive/ Getty Images

p.159 © MediaPunch Inc/Alamy Stock Photo

p.189 © Luke Durda/Alamy Stock Photo

p.216 © Dylan Martinez

p.224 © William Barton/Alamy stock photo

All other images supplied courtesy of the author.

While every effort has been made to trace the owners of copyright material reproduced herein and secure permissions, the publishers would like to apologise for any omissions and will be pleased to incorporate missing acknowledgements in any future edition of this book.